Kentucky Crafts

Dear Alan,

Enjoy the crafts of
Kentucky!

Phyllis George

Phyllis George

Kentucky Crafts

Handmade and Heartfelt

CROWN PUBLISHERS, INC. NEW YORK

Published by Crown Publishers, Inc.,
201 East 50th Street, New York, New York 10022

CROWN is a trademark of Crown Publishers, Inc.
Manufactured in Japan
Library of Congress Cataloging-in-Publication Data

George, Phyllis
Kentucky crafts : handmade and heartfelt /
by Phyllis George. — 1st ed.
p.   cm.
1. Decorative arts—Kentucky.   2. Handicraft—Kentucky.
3. Artisans—Kentucky—Biography.   I. Title.
NK835.K4B76   1989   745'.092'2—dc19
[B]
89-1147
ISBN 0-517-57327-X
10 9 8 7 6 5 4 3 2 1
First Edition

REMINISCENT OF A ROCKY TOP SEASON

Knoxville designer Molly Bland loves using decorations that extend beyond the holidays. "I was inspired by a friend to use a combination of lemon leaf and dried artichokes," she explains. "I prefer to enjoy decorations year-round, as do many of my clients."

A layer of sphagnum moss tucked into the vines of the wreath acts as an anchor for the natural ornaments. Dusting the tips of the vegetables and freeze-dried blackberries with gold paint gives the wreath a festive touch. Pheasant feathers, placed throughout, add interest and depth to the design while echoing a back-to-nature theme.

...ntucky,
...whose spirit
...follow;

...ob George,
...ished in me
...respect
...;

...partner,
...ages me

...nd Pamela,
...Kentucky crafts
...ch legacy
...ook.

Contents

Foreword

In 1981 when Phyllis George Brown, on behalf of the Kentucky Department of the Arts, asked me to establish and head a new statewide program called the Kentucky Art and Craft Foundation, I didn't hesitate. I knew that I had two dynamos backing me up: Phyllis and Lois Mateus Musselman, then State Arts Commissioner. It was clear to me how much they cared about the success of the new organization. Of course, there was no staff, no board, no budget, no gallery, no program. That was going to be my job! But I felt we could do it. The tradition of craft in Kentucky has a long and illustrious history, and the moment had arrived for an organization that would help bring it into focus.

Soon we formed a dynamic board, drawing from all over the state. We were off to a good start through the indefatigable promotional efforts of Phyllis to bring Kentucky crafts to the top department stores in New York, Los Angeles, and Chicago. There were glamorous openings of Kentucky craft boutiques in Bloomingdale's and Neiman-Marcus. Overnight there was a new audience, and orders for Kentucky crafts started flying in. Soon we were organizing workshops for craftspeople, giving help with the business end of things. Some became so financially independent that they no longer needed our help. That's the way we wanted it. In 1983 we were able to employ a part-time staff person, and we began a newsletter, *Made in Kentucky*, which now has a subscription list of 2,800.

The following year we opened a permanent gallery and shop in downtown Louisville. That was a momentous commitment by our board, but it has paid off in so many ways that it is hard to imagine what we were like before. We had the opportunity to show and tell the Kentucky craft story to the public at large, to create a real center where people could come and see the best and most innovative crafts being produced in the state. Soon after the gallery opened, we added a full-time executive director for our organization and later a full-time curator for the gallery. Shows and catalogs produced with corporate support became regular features of the gallery. Coverage in the media helped sharpen our focus and bring in new audiences.

The list of exhibits over the last four years is lengthy, but some of our most innovative and popular have been "Art and Architecture," in which Kentucky architects were teamed with craftspeople; our now-famous "Chair Show," which traveled extensively; a show of folding screens, each especially designed by a Kentucky artist; and "See the Light," based on crafted lamps. On other occasions we have exhibited puppets or walking sticks or fantasies in glass. At the same time our shop did about $250,000 in business in 1988. Our audience comes to see *and* buy.

Our next move will be to open an additional floor of gallery space where large-scale pieces of craft furniture can be shown. It is hard to believe that we have grown so much from the germ of an idea eight years ago. But our focus remains the same — to assist the Kentucky craftsperson to develop both talent and career.

The craft movement throughout America is still gaining momentum. The opening of the new American Craft Museum in New York in 1986 and the growing number of fine-art galleries in major cities showing crafts have brought new prominence to the movement. Yet for all this, craft remains a regional phenomenon rooted in places like Kentucky. We can be proud that we are in the forefront in giving craft artists the support they must have to rise to the top and achieve national recognition.

MARY NORTON SHANDS
President
Kentucky Art and Craft Foundation

I n t r o d u c t i o n

Kentucky craft is a living tradition. I am proud to be able to introduce you to some of the hearts and hands behind the works of art known as Kentucky Crafts.

We are blessed in Kentucky with hundreds of wonderful artists, artisans, and craftspeople, more than we could possibly feature in this one book. This volume contains the stories of forty-eight of Kentucky's fine artists and craftspeople and their families. They are stories that must be told, because they link us all to our past, our roots, our ancestors. As you will see from the beautiful photographs and personal stories in this book, this is a legacy worth showing and preserving.

I have spent the last ten years of my life on a true "crafts odyssey" in Kentucky. Discovering and collecting crafts has become more than just a hobby for me — it is my passion. Getting to know the people who hand make these beautiful things — talking with them about their work, their dreams, and their lives — has been one of the most enriching experiences of my life.

I have traveled from the mountains and hollows of eastern Kentucky to the lake regions of western Kentucky, from the largest cities and suburbs of Louisville and Lexington to the smallest farms in the Bluegrass to find these artisans. Some work out of sophisticated fine-arts studios at state universities, others work at homes so remote that you need a vehicle with four-wheel drive to reach them. Many work in converted garages and basement workshops, often late into the evenings after working a day job. Some weave, others quilt; some carve, others hammer; some throw pots, others

paint. They are of all ages, all types, and all backgrounds, but they have one thing in common — they represent a vanishing breed of artists and craftspeople who, often at great personal and family sacrifice, have chosen lives dedicated to preserving the Kentucky tradition of making things by hand.

I first came to Kentucky as a newly-wed in the spring of 1979. My new husband, John Y. Brown, Jr., and I flew to Kentucky to announce his candidacy for governor right after our honeymoon. I felt an immediate emotional attachment to Kentucky and particularly to its craftspeople who had a purity, honesty, and earthiness about them that I had rarely found in the entertainment business. They seemed to possess the same pioneer spirit that had driven many of their forefathers across the mountains to create new lives for themselves in Kentucky. Family roots and tradition are important to these people. As you will read in their stories, many of them learned their crafts from their parents and grandparents and are passing them on to their sons and daughters. Almost all are supported by strong families — often spouses — who get involved as helpers, business managers, and sellers. The crafts business in Kentucky is almost always a business that involves whole families.

These people are the keepers of the skills and talents that built American life as we now know it. Their stories are an inspiration to all of us who live fast-paced lives in a high-tech society and who need reminders now and then of where we came from and of what is important and lasting in life.

My own love affair with Kentucky crafts really began during John's campaign for governor. Life on the campaign trail was exhausting, but it was a perfect introduction for me to the breathtaking beauty of my newly adopted state. Much of our traveling was done, by necessity, in a helicopter. From the air, Kentucky resembled a beautiful patchwork quilt. It was so different from my home state of Texas. I fell in love with the bluegrass, the mountains, the manicured horse farms with their white fences and prancing thoroughbreds. As our helicopter landed in each small town, John would rush off to make speeches and have campaign meetings, and I would often have a chance to sneak away to wander through the towns to meet people. "Wandering" usually meant shopping and I found myself building a collection of "keepsakes"

— quilts of all colors and designs, baskets of all shapes and sizes, hand-carved ducks and figures, Shaker boxes, unique hand-painted gourds, pottery. I would stack all my new treasures into the helicopter, and off we would go to the next destination. As I looked at my growing collection of crafts, I was impressed with the skill and patience that went into hand making them and with the artists' dedication to preserving traditions and talents.

My enthusiasm for my new home and for the crafts I was discovering really intensified after John was elected governor. I had to travel to New York on weekends for my job as a network sportscaster and, in my spare time, I would take long walks up Madison and Fifth Avenues and go into some of the shops that carried handmade items. I can remember being shocked that most of the crafts sold were made in Hong Kong, Japan, Haiti, Tahiti — all places outside America. Many were not as interesting or as beautiful as the handmade things I had seen on my travels around

Kentucky. I made a promise to myself that one way or another, as First Lady of Kentucky, I would commit myself to helping our craftspeople find new places to show and sell their wonderful things. Thus began my mission to promote Kentucky crafts.

Things began to come together when my good friend, Lois Mateus Musselman, who was then Kentucky's Commissioner of the Arts and who is now senior vice-president of Brown-Forman Corporation, helped me convince John, as governor, to establish a crafts promotion program within her department of state government. At the same time, I started spreading the word about Kentucky crafts everywhere I traveled. I sent a variety of crafts to my friends all across the country — beautiful shawls and baby blankets from Churchill Weavers, ducks hand-carved ("with God's help") by Tim Hall, baskets from Curtis Alvey's Basket Barn filled with Kentucky delicacies. Each time, I felt I was giving my friends heirlooms, pieces of art that could be treasured and passed down through generations. The Department of the Arts started sponsoring new crafts markets, which attracted craftspeople waiting for just such opportunities to show off their wares. Several hundred of the craftspeople contributed handmade ornaments to the Christmas tree in the Capitol Rotunda the first year. Gift and specialty buyers from around the region started coming to our markets, too, and buying our products. Word spread fast — and widely — and before long we were contacted for national television interviews and for stories and full-length features in national magazines such as *Redbook, Family Circle, Better Homes and Gardens, Country Living,* and *Architectural Digest.*

Our biggest promotional opportunity came, however, when I attended the Democratic National Convention in New York in the summer of 1980. Marvin Traub, the chairman of Bloomingdale's, hosted a beautiful party in his store for governors' wives. At the time, Bloomingdale's was showcasing a collection of art objects from China. Marvin would point proudly to a unique piece in his China collection and I would find myself saying, "But Marvin, you just have to see the beautiful pottery being hand-fired by four generations of one family in a barn in Bybee, Kentucky," or "That Chinese tapestry is lovely, Marvin, but I've discovered extraordinary hand-sewn quilts in Kentucky that make beautiful wall hangings, and they're made here in America!"

I had a hard time, obviously, curtailing my enthusiasm. But Marvin Traub is a retailing wizard, and I think he realized, as we talked, that the timing was right for Bloomingdale's to participate in a made-in-America promotion. The mood of the country at the time was swinging back to basic, traditional values and a rebirth of appreciation for a simple, down-to-earth lifestyle.

Marvin responded enthusiastically to our idea for a Kentucky Crafts promotion, and within a few days, Lois was on a plane to New York with a Bybee bowl in her lap and an assortment of other crafts in her dufflebag. The buyers at Bloomingdale's loved what they saw and by early October had dispatched scouts to Kentucky to gather merchandise for the show. They crisscrossed the state in a helicopter, then returned with a pickup truck that they filled with Marvin Finn's whimsical folk art figures, quilts from David · Appalachian crafts, place settings of Bybee pottery, and many of the other beautiful crafts featured in this book.

When the "Oh! Kentucky" boutique opened up at Bloomingdale's in March of 1981 to the music of Homer Ledford's bluegrass band, Kentucky's art and crafts revival was launched. We were an instant hit in Manhattan. The *New York Times* and Associated Press lauded Kentucky's support and promotion of things made by hand. Many of the items in the boutique sold out in the first week. One-of-a-kind pieces such as the lovely bent-twig loveseat — later

copied by everyone — became collectors' items in the homes of the lucky people who rushed in to discover them at Bloomingdale's.

Our success at Bloomingdale's was immediately noted by other major department stores. Neiman-Marcus immediately made plans for their buyers to visit Kentucky to shop for boutique items for their posh Beverly Hills store.

Things really snowballed from there — Marshall Field's, Bullocks, and others featured "Kentucky Country Chic" promotions. I even toted Kentucky crafts with me on a trip to Japan with my husband and, after they saw our beautiful things, Japan's biggest department store, Takashimaya, launched a "Made-in-America" store promotion featuring Kentucky crafts. We started making semi-annual visits to the New York gift shows. Markets exploded, which meant that more and more sales opportunities opened up for Kentucky's artists and craftspeople.

The most beautiful thing about the whole success story is that, in each instance, all we had to do was crack the door open — the crafts and the wonderful people who made them sold themselves every time.

The attention we brought Kentucky crafts helped foster a new appreciation for using handmade, one-of-a-kind creations in American furnishing and decorating as well. People were very happy to be able to buy unique, handmade items instead of machine-made replicas. The Kentucky Governor's Mansion, which we completely restored when we lived there, and our private home in Lexington, Kentucky, Cave Hill Place, were each featured in *Architectural Digest* while John was governor. Each article emphasized the ease with which we were able to incorporate Kentucky crafts into our decorating schemes. The eclectic effect of sprinkling handmade Kentucky crafts among antiques and porcelains and alongside silver picture frames on quilt-covered tables added warmth and a simple elegance to each of our rooms.

Perhaps the most important thing to come out of the resurgence of the craft movement, however, was the recognition and respect that it brought to Kentucky's arti-sans, many of

whom had thought about abandoning their talents and their homes when the farm economy slumped and the coal mines closed. That little boost in family income, when markets started opening up, helped save a few farms, we've been told, and helped establish viable cottage industries and co-ops in the mountains to help support the families with so few other opportunities for income.

The new recognition and respect strengthened the craftspeople's determination to continue their work. As many of them will tell you in the pages to follow, they are committed to continuing the legacy of hand-making crafts. They refuse to mechanize their production to increase volume and sales. Their real satisfaction comes from perfecting their craft and stretching their talents in new directions. Their patience and concentration and attention to detail continue to impress me. They are totally dedicated to their crafts, and it shows.

Over the years, I have received volumes of beautiful letters from the friends I have made in my crafts travels. I stay in touch with many of them by attending crafts fairs held each year throughout Kentucky. But working on this book gave me a rare opportunity to visit some of them in their homes and studios, and

this time I got to tour Kentucky on the ground. I traveled with my dear friend Carol Butler, who was John's general counsel when he was governor. We logged hundreds of miles in her big, blue station wagon, which served us well as we filled it up with "souvenirs" from our journeys. Our trips and, especially, our visits with the people in this book were inspirational. I fell in love with Kentucky and its remarkable craftspeople all over again and I understood, once again, why my years acting as a sort of godmother to Kentucky crafts have been some of the most satisfying of my life.

I am happy that Kentucky's commitment to the promotion of its crafts has been continued by each governor's administration since John's. I am particularly proud of the real day-to-day work being carried on by the private, nonprofit Kentucky Art and Craft Foundation. We established the Foundation in 1981, and John appointed wonderful Mary Norton Shands as its chairman. Mary and her husband, Al, a member of the board of the American Craft Council headquartered in New York, are known and respected nationally for their knowledge and dedication to the promotion of American crafts and folk art. Together they have spearheaded the Foundation's efforts to locate and promote Kentucky artists and craftspeople. With their continuing commitment and support, the

Foundation has been able to open the Kentucky Art and Craft Gallery on Main Street in downtown Louisville, which showcases the best and latest in hand-made Kentucky art and crafts. Because of its proximity to major hotels and the Kentucky Center for the Arts, it has become one of the most popular shopping spots in downtown Louisville.

The Foundation also serves as a great source of information on Kentucky crafts and is an important link between buyers and the craftspeople, many of whom live in remote corners of the state. I encourage any reader who wants more information on the artists or crafts items featured in this book to contact the Foundation for assistance. Whether you are a serious crafts collector or someone just looking for a unique gift for a special occasion, I assure you that one call will whet your appetite for the enormous pleasure that comes from owning or giving a handmade Kentucky craft.

This book has been written to document the stories of some of the people behind Kentucky crafts. They are the real magic behind our success story. I am truly grateful to Crown Publishers, particularly to Senior Vice President Michelle Sidrane, and to Carol and Bill Butler, Bill Strode, and Ken Hayden of Harmony House Publishers in Louisville, the producers of this book, for sharing my vision and enthusiasm, and for helping me to capture this important moment in Kentucky's crafts history.

Join me now to meet some of the truly remarkable people creating the phenomenon called Kentucky Crafts.

Wood and Furniture

Roger Blair

Wood carver Roger Blair has become well known in Kentucky crafts circles in the last five years, and in national circles, too, since so many prominent people are now proud owners of Roger's carved birds, fish, horses, and other wildlife. His presence at crafts shows and in stores lead people to believe Roger carves for a living, but that's not the case. He is a full-time farmer in Campbellsville, Kentucky. He and his family lead the time-honored farm life, raising crops and dairy cattle, putting in a full day's work. But when time is available,

Roger can be found in his guest house/ studio, carving one of the hundreds of finely detailed still lifes of animals he completes each year.

Roger doesn't do all his work in the studio, however. For carvers like Roger, having a knife in your pocket means you can always do a little carving wherever you are, even when you have only a few minutes. While Roger's dairy cows are on the milking machines, for instance, Roger uses the time to sit back and rough out a figure of a thoroughbred or to put the finishing touches on a smallmouth bass taking a lure.

Carving is a skill that has brought Roger critical acclaim and a measure of fame, but as we sat talking on a hot summer day in his studio, I felt that his love of carving and his life on the farm were the things he cared most about. In that way he is like most of the craftspeople in Kentucky. As he puts it, "You want to carve something that comes from the heart and not something that you're trying to do thinking people will buy it. This is not a job with me."

I 've been whittling ever since I was big enough to use a knife. I was always fascinated with wood. I got knives for Christmas and I started carving birds and deer and little ground squirrels. I carved for five years. I didn't try to sell them. I just made them and then stopped because I'd run out of places to put them. People were always interested in them at Christmas or for birthdays. And it just started getting bigger. Then I heard these people say, "You ought to go to this crafts fair in Louisville." So I went up there, and I sold four hundred dollars worth of my things just like that. That was good. So, I went back the next year to sell a little more. People start looking for you to come back.

I'm self-taught. I just picked up carving one day. I saw an old man in Indiana carving a bird. I always wanted to do it. I

OPPOSITE: "I really work two jobs. I can carve while I'm milking our cows, and that's how I can do as much as I can do in wood carving."

just never did take the time to try, because I didn't think I could. I was putting up an electric fence and there was this little sawed-off fence post. So I said, "I'm going to try carving an owl out of that." That was my first piece. Then I said, "I'm gonna try me a bigger one," so I got a chunk of walnut. I got old chisels and a hammer, and I had the handle beat off the chisel within half a day. I was doing full-sized birds within three months. It was just like I tapped into something that I didn't even know I could do. It just came so easy.

I farm with my brothers and my dad. We mow hay, raise tobacco, and do everything else there is to do with farming. We all work together and that gives me a chance to go to crafts fairs. Farming has helped, in that you're out there in the field every day. You can see all these little birds that people in their studios don't see. And when I'm out there, I can see all that — how little birds feed their young, for example. I saw this redtail catch a cowsnake, you know, and I'm thinking, it'd be a good scene to carve — have the hawk's neck feathers flared out — something with excitement. So many carvers would have the snake already caught. They don't give him any chance of getting away, you know. Most of the time they do get away. I carved the scene with the action stopped just at the peak of excitement, where you don't know if the hawk won, or the snake got away.

If all this ended tomorrow, I'd keep doing it anyway. It's too much fun. It's in my blood, I guess.

"It's like this jockey right here. He's wanting that horse to really go, and the horse has got his nostrils out, and the man's saying, 'Go ! Go !' "

"One thing I do different from other carvers is I don't do glass eyes. I carve the eyes. The art of it is bringing life into the wooden eyes, because the eyes have everything to do with it. They've got that little sparkle. You can have the best carving in the world, and if the eyes are wrong, it's ruined."

Homer Ledford

I just love Homer Ledford. He's tall and lanky and he's been a favorite of mine for a long time. He comes to my house often to play and sing at get-togethers and birthday parties, and I see him at crafts fairs every year. Last year at the spring crafts fair at Berea he taught me how to play one of the dulcimers he's so famous for.

Homer is legendary in music circles as a performer who can play ten different folk instruments, either solo or as part of The Cabin Creek Band. The City of Winchester, Kentucky, honored Homer by naming its annual bluegrass festival after him.

In crafts circles he is also known as a master builder of dulcimers, guitars, and banjos. He has made instruments for many country and western and bluegrass performers, and for private collectors who don't play professionally but admire the workmanship in his instruments. "Some of my

customers are professional musicians," he says, "and some aren't. This one fellow, a lawyer, had fifteen Martin guitars and he wanted me to make him one. I said, 'I can sell you another Martin cheaper than I can make you a guitar, plus it's going to take some time.' He said, 'That's all right, I'd really like to have one of yours.' So I made him one."

Homer works in an elaborate workshop in the basement of his home. I caught up with him there and learned about his life as a Kentucky musician and craftsman.

W hen I was a kid, there were some nice fellows who went through the mountains every year. They were like two preachers, I guess. One played the fiddle and the other the guitar. They would come and stay with you as long as you'd keep them. Music was in big demand through the mountains. On Saturday nights we'd roll back the rug and have a good

square dance. It didn't matter if you had a guitar player or not, but that fiddler was important. I can remember sitting on the bed and thinking how great that fiddle sounded to me. I always wanted one. That was a great inspiration, and how I got keyed up on music.

Well, since I was kind of handy with my hands, I started trying to make instruments. We had lots of Sears catalogs and they had pictures of these fiddles, so I just made one. This was somewhere around 1942, when I was in high school.

The dulcimer came along, for me, in 1946. I never thought much of the dulcimer. By that time I had learned to play a guitar and, you know, a guitar is a complicated instrument with a big sound. I just kind of laughed at the dulcimer. I never really knew that I was going to make them. But Jean Ritchie had gone to New York and she was playing her dulcimer for the kids there. And the dulcimer just caught on. The New Yorkers really flipped over that thing. They just kept asking where they could find a dulcimer. I learned about them from ones

"I've made a couple of electric guitars, but I really don't like electric music. I like acoustic music. I call it 'real music.'"

I had seen, and I started making them. Now I have made 5,196 of them. I've never had any help on any of them, except from my son when he was younger and still home. I like to do it all by myself, really.

I made my own guitar back last July. I finished it up and it's at a show up there in Louisville. I thought it might win a prize, but no way. I don't win prizes. You see, I'm not making art forms. If you are into art forms and sculpture, you'll win prizes. That's the way it works. You don't win prizes in guitars unless you're in a crafts show or something like that where they are looking at your carving, your craftsmanship, construction, design, the whole works. I won on my banjo in Cincinnati. I brought the same banjo down to a Louisville show last year and didn't get a look. So, it's just one of those things. I never go with the idea of really winning much anyway as it is. I did win over here at the Berea fair on my dulcimer, though. Craftsmen voted on that. They know what crafts are, and they appreciated what I had made. I won out over all of them. But in these art shows, forget it.

I don't think I could improve the classic guitar body style and that's why I won't touch it. I could design different instruments all day. I've even thought about it. But I've thought also, I don't have a lot of time to do all that. I intend to make just so many dulcimers and guitars and banjos. I have to go with what I have time to do. I would dearly love to design, redesign, and make new things every day because that's where it is fun, really. I get all excited just making guitars. I really can't wait to get to the shop in the mornings. And I won't let up until my wife hollers lunch, or it's time to come in to supper.

"I've not been willing to take an apprentice, because I think we would just be falling over each other in the shop. I just enjoy making the whole thing."

Virginia Petty

Virginia Petty could have been born a hundred years ago. This lovely lady displays the kinds of talents that might have been commonplace on the wild frontier. She handles all kinds of firearms easily and well; she knows her way around the woods; she can sharpen and use a knife; she can farm; she can hunt and fish; she has the strength that comes from a lifetime of old-fashioned work.

This kind of self-reliance is right in step with the craft that has made her well known in Kentucky — she makes a variety of wooden spoons, ladles, scoops, and utensils, all hand carved from wood salvaged from the beams and floor joists of buildings as much as two hundred years old. She sells these pieces under the name of The Whistlin' Whittler, a moniker she started using when

she wasn't sure if anyone would buy hand-carved things from a woman. Virginia is now known and loved by many people all across Kentucky.

She has a real camaraderie with other Kentucky craftspeople and has expanded her own talents by spending time with them at crafts markets. She now dabbles in dulcimers, Shaker boxes, baskets — in fact, she recently wove a beautiful random-weave basket while she was sitting in a field watching a calf being born.

Virginia and her husband, Paul, and son, Brack, live on 155 acres in western Kentucky, where they grow corn, tobacco, and alfalfa and raise pigs and cattle. It's a lot of work, but Virginia loves the life, especially when the fish are biting down at the bass pond.

I spent a lovely morning with her around the kitchen table, talking about life on Three Forks Flat Rock Road, off Smith's Grove-Scottsdale Road, in the center of Dead Dog Hollow, Little Elk, and Spread Elm.

I have to be honest with you. If it hadn't been for the crafts markets opening up here in Kentucky in 1980, and my husband's supporting my selling all these things, he and I might've lost this farm. The extra money we were able to bring home from our sales at those markets literally kept us from going under back then. We are so grateful things happened when they did.

I don't know whether I'm a whittler or a woodcarver. A whittler is someone who aimlessly makes shavings, not having any idea what he's making. A woodcarver has a direction he wants to go. He has a thing he intends to produce and he produces it. Actually, I am the Whistling Woodcarver. I don't do much just plain whittling anymore. I just don't have time for it.

I don't like to sell at shows. I like for someone to come in and say, "Oh, I like this," and then I tell them the story behind the piece and they say, "Oh, you're the one

who does it." And I say, "Yes, I am, and I've got the calluses to prove it." So often, when my husband goes with me to a show, if he is in the booth with me, people will ignore me entirely and talk to my husband. And he'll say, "I don't do it, she does." But if I go off and leave him in the booth and someone says, "You do lovely work," he just says thanks. He gets tired of explaining.

I had support from my mother. She pushed me, encouraged me. And then my husband not only encouraged me, he finally shoved me. It was "Honey, go do it. You can do it. It's a great opportunity. Do it." And I probably wouldn't have done it without him.

Someone asked me one time why I didn't make measuring cups and spoons. I said I didn't want to do that. I don't want to have to be exact on anything. I want to play.

I want the slight, uneven cutting marks and hammer marks on my utensils. If it looks machine made, I've destroyed one very good reason for someone to buy it.

I buff my utensils with paraffin. Wood doesn't need any protection. I buff them simply to bring out the color. Using them with food does them good, the oils in shortening and all. As a matter of fact, you're supposed to rub them down with liquid shortening every now and then.

When I was a kid, I had great plans to be

"I want the slight, uneven cutting marks and hammer marks on my utensils."

an electrical engineer. I even had a scholarship to go to Tennessee Tech. But in the meantime, I met my future husband, and I didn't want to leave town, so I blew it. Yeah, I did. I blew it. But I'm a whole lot happier for having done it that way. I don't think I would have been a very happy electrical engineer.

Never in my wildest dreams did it occur to me that I would wind up in a book. If you're sharing my story, and if the reader gets something from reading the story, then they have a part of me. I like that.

 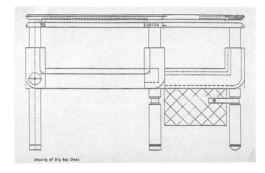 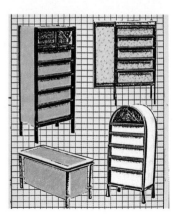

Len Wujcik

Since early childhood in Pennsylvania, Len Wujcik has been fascinated with making things — "assembling materials" to be exact. He has worked in wood, metal, stone, glass, ceramics, plastic, fabric — every conceivable material. But he has found a unique way to combine his talents in his current careers as a furniture designer and instructor of three-dimensional design at the University of Kentucky.

Len will call himself an "applied artist" — not a craftsperson — but he will quickly add that his pieces, though "artfully expressive," are primarily functional; "not esoteric enough to be seen as fine art."

We finally decided his pieces could best be described as "collage furniture." His

unique technique of assembling an odd assortment of materials to produce one-of-a-kind pieces of functional art is the perfect culmination of the "collage" of talents Len has developed throughout his creative life.

The day we visited Len, he took us on a tour of the home-studio he is renovating in Lexington, showed us some of his finest design pieces, then treated us to some mean Cajun tunes on the accordion. A "collage" of talents — all functional, of course.

I grew up near Wilkes-Barre, Pennsylvania, and I guess my interest in building comes from my environment. Both of my parents are from large, close, ethnic families. We lived in half of a double block on what is called "Wujciks' Alley." When somebody needed work done on their house, no matter what the job, you didn't hire anybody to do it, you did it yourself or family came and helped. Even early on, we built little bunks out back as architectural projects. That's how I started.

I have always had this fascination with materials and how an assembly of the materials would then read as an object, as a finished construction. Even now, the investigation of material and process is primary to the form — the main impetus to the form that you see. I am not a romantic about materials. I will use any material that suits me. I can see wood as "stuff," or I can see the natural beauty of wood and enjoy the grain pattern and colors in it. I'll see it either way. It depends on what the project is.

I respect traditional techniques. But I'm terrible because I'm a heretic in many ways. I will do a traditional piece straight down to the raised-panel drawer bottoms and the pined mortise and tenons, and I have done them. A traditional piece allows me to hone skills, to rediscover traditional techniques of assembly, to rediscover traditional surfaces. In doing a reproduction you are, in many ways, forced to do certain things, where, in a contemporary piece, I can be quite lazy and I can design my way around

problems — and the truth is that's what I and other designers often do.

I don't believe that furniture necessarily has to have roots in traditional objects, because traditional objects use traditional materials. You do not need the skills in doing a contemporary piece out of glass that you would need in doing one out of wood; neither do they need to share a basic understanding. They are two unique materials. They work distinctly differently. I don't believe that somebody needs to pass through a traditional realm to do contemporary furniture.

In designing I am relentless in my questioning, taking everything into consideration. I have lost students who insist that their first idea is the one that they want to make. When I start a project, typically I will pack it with so many alternatives that I have to go back and sort through and reject ideas just to come up with what I feel works best . I think a lot of people have a misconception of what it means to design. They see it as only ac-

"Some people have said, 'How did you make the joints to have it all look so cocked?' Like I made complicated joints to do it. All I did was raise the end."

cepting ideas. Design is a process in which one does more rejecting than accepting. I think having a historic, cultural, and technical understanding of furniture is all valuable. But I don't see it as an absolute criterion to doing contemporary work.

I don't call my work art. I practice the applied art of furniture design. Like a fine art, through formal visual and structural language, I use the work to be personally expressive, but in the final summation it is the applied art of furniture making. It has a functional purpose.

I think of myself as a three-dimensional designer. In the world of "isms" I would call my style "Expressive Rationalism." I don't limit my materials as some artisans do. Instead, I enjoy the challenge and fun of collaging mixed materials, at human scale, to produce furniture forms. That's why I do furniture.

T i m   H a l l

Ten years ago, Tim Hall found his life's work — carving incredibly lifelike ducks, geese, and birds — and since then his rise to craft stardom has been swift. He is now one of Kentucky's most famous artisans, having been featured on many wildlife television shows, in countless newspapers, in national magazines, and at international carving shows and demonstrations.

Like many other craftsmen, Tim's hobby became a business when people first saw his waterfowl carvings and started buying them. Tim believes this turn of events was not accidental. "God has always worked out things for me in my life," he says. "That's why I always sign the bottom of my ducks, 'Made by Tim Hall with God's help.' It's my way of witnessing people, telling them what the Lord has done for me."

Tim has been a favorite of mine for years. I collect his ducks and have a personally autographed one on the mantel in my den at Cave Hill Place.

His love of life and the outdoors gives him a warm and sunny personality that is contagious. "I'm the luckiest guy in the world," he says, "doing something I love for a living."

I went to see Tim at his home in Ravenna, Kentucky, near the Kentucky River. In his cozy woodcarving studio beside the house, he told me about how his new career got started.

I used to be a carpenter. And I just thought I'd try carving a bird one day. Somebody bought it and I thought maybe I could make a living like this. It turns out I have, but I always try to give the Lord credit for it. He's worked it out for me to make a living out of it.

I'm self-taught. On the first couple of birds, everything went wrong. Of course, my mom would say, "Oh, those are great." But I knew better right off. And I just tried to improve them every time.

I don't have a model for everything I make. I do have a few mounted ducks that I use for reference. But the best references are photographs. There are a lot of books that have excellent photographs, and I always get outdoor magazines. I can, a lot of times, make a pattern just from a magazine. Of course, I have to have enough knowledge to pick up the other views.

You can't rely on mounts too much, because they can be inaccurate. And a lot of things about them change, like the bills. You're better off with a good photograph. That's a lot of it, plus just knowing the bird. I've got some duck wings I figured I'd keep. Most ducks have ten primary feathers and ten secondary feathers and I know the general shape of them. I just compute those dimensions to scale.

Sometimes this work is hard on my hands. I'm sitting here producing what I like to think of as art work, and you would think it's more of a factory-type thing, because I'm doing it constantly, you know. Each little feather is burned in with the wood burner. If you sit and do that all day long, at the end of the day, it does get to your hands. And painting is real tedious, holding a small brush all day. On some of those ones that fly, I'll have over a hundred hours in just the work. Not the studying, you know, drawing it up or anything. I've gotten to where I just keep on adding to what I do for the year. Last year I did a

hundred and five carvings. That was the most I'd ever done.

In the early years, I was really kind of depressed about the whole thing, and I was about to give it up. I wasn't selling much. But I got this letter in the mail about this thing the state was getting going — a crafts show over at the Horse Park. I said to myself, "I'm going to give it one more shot,

and if I do well, fine. And if I don't, I'm going to do something to take care of my family." It so happened that that show was real good for me. I sold about everything that I took. Without that, I probably would never have quit my carpentry job. It was a well-paying job. It was some security, I guess you could say. It took a lot to leave.

I think I've found the right thing, because

"Birds are my specialty. I'm a bird watcher. Duck hunter. I love the birds."

I just love it. It's not like a job to me. At one time I thought, "What are you doing?" But I won't again. The Lord has always worked it out for me. So I want to stay in His will, whatever that is. I'm happy with it, and it suits me if I can just do this the rest of my life. He's blessed me so far.

*"The reason I like to do these
things is to share them with the
people who don't get to see them. I
get to see a lot of stuff out in the
woods, and most people don't
really get to see those things and
appreciate them. I guess that's
part of the satisfaction I get."*

J a c k   J o h n s o n

Like many other Kentucky crafts-men, Jack Johnson stumbled upon the craft that has made him famous. He wasn't looking for fame — he was just pursuing a hobby to pass the time after work. But the hobby — making Shaker boxes in a traditional but unique way — has become a thriving business, and Jack has discovered that he possesses an amazing affinity for wood, after a lifetime of being unaware of his talents.

I'm proud to say that I had something to do with Jack's success. I bought the first Shaker box Jack ever made. I didn't know it at the time. I assumed, looking at his workmanship, that Jack had been making them all his life. I also didn't know that my purchase would encourage Jack to continue making Shaker boxes, even though he had been thinking about experimenting with other things.

Jack has lived in Morehead, Kentucky, all

his life, and lives now on the same street where he grew up. It's a quiet country lane near cornfields and woods. It's a great spot for gathering wood and pursuing a craft at a pace of one's own choosing. Although the popularity of his creations has made time demands that keep him from enjoying the small-town life he's used to, Jack still enjoys doing the work, and I'm so glad.

In 1978 I was making wooden pitchforks just for fun that turned out pretty good, so I started to experiment. I made ladder-back chairs, hoes, children's rockers. I made one Shaker box and took it to Frankfort to a crafts fair that the state was sponsoring. You bought the first one, Phyllis, and gave it to Robert Redford for a gift. I think he was in Kentucky making a movie. That kind of gave my business a boost.

I enjoy making Shaker boxes. It gets me away from the computers and everything at the phone company. I've been working there since 1966. I work in the central office. Working with wood and working at the telephone company is like the difference between daylight and dark.

It's fun making Shaker boxes, but when you get real busy it's not quite as much fun. It's more fun to me to experiment around. I'd like to have time to make some chairs and some white-oak baskets. I love to make white-oak baskets. I also love to put hickory bark in chairs. But everyone loves the boxes, so I keep making them.

I just use regular tools: a hatchet, shaving horse, spoke shave, drill. Now I have a hand plane so that I can plane them down quicker. I use it because, to produce, you have to get them done quicker. I use pad sanders, too, but nothing fancy or special.

Almost every tree acts different when you fool with it. Oaks are real bad — every one you cut is different. Maple isn't quite as bad. I cut a white oak once, just the right size for a basket, and it looked perfect. I brought it down here and started splitting it and I couldn't do anything with it. It wouldn't cooperate at all. You may bring home one that will split right up and then the next one you bring home may be different.

I've cut just about every good slick-bark maple around here. That's the very best kind. They're hard to find anymore, I've cut so many of them. I just go pick me out a

tree somewhere, anywhere from ten to fifteen inches in diameter, something that's good and straight with no limbs. I can get a piece five or six feet long with no knots, and start splitting just like you would shingles. It has to be green wood, and it has to stay green while I'm using it. I have to keep it wrapped in plastic to keep it from drying out on me.

I never really thought I'd be a craftsman in woodworking. Actually, I never even thought about woodworking. I just got interested in the natural stuff.

I'm probably getting better at Shaker boxes. I'm not really getting better at any of the other things that involve wood because I'm not able to do it. Experience is the best teacher.

If I want something bad enough, I'll try to make it. I don't usually collect that many

crafts from other people. Mostly what I buy are pottery things. I like the old stone pottery cups. Not to take anything from anybody else, but I like to try to make things I want, just to see if I can do it.

We've lost a lot of arts but some have been kept alive, like how to build log cabins. I don't think making Shaker boxes is a lost art. There are quite a few people making them around the country. I demonstrate and try to answer questions but I don't teach. We get a lot of people from different states in the Northeast down here wanting to know how I make the boxes. They've never seen anything like it.

I don't think that just Kentuckians are good at crafts — I think it's more of a generation thing. When I was growing up we had to provide for ourselves; we only bought what we had to. I think a lot of

"I've learned a lot of this myself. When you look in a book, sometimes you find you don't understand it. So you just start, and eventually you get it right."

people in other states are like that, too. But city kids, for example, aren't going to learn how to make things like someone who's grown up on a farm.

I'd like to be able to live off what I retire on, and anything else would be extra. I wouldn't want to have to do woodwork. I love it and enjoy it but I wouldn't want to have to do it every day — it's hard work.

I guess most of the people around here know about me. I've had a couple of write-ups in the Morehead paper. I always thought that a person could do whatever they set their mind to. So if I can do it, there's no reason you or someone else couldn't learn it, too.

"When I start on the boxes, I saw out twenty-five or thirty, and get my material ready for the sides. I work on a whole bunch at a time; I won't make just one or two."

W a r r e n   M a y

Woodworker Warren May is not only one of the most talented dulcimer makers in this part of the country, he is also one of the finest furniture makers.

I have come to know Warren over the years I've been in Kentucky and to respect him as a dedicated family man who not only has made a name for himself in woodworking circles across America, but who has spent a great amount of his own time and considerable energy promoting Kentucky craftspeople, primarily those working around Berea, Kentucky.

Warren May's Upstairs Gallery was one of the first crafts shops I found when I first moved to Kentucky. It showcased the works of over one hundred Kentucky craftspeople. I remember sneaking a few private moments from a gubernatorial campaign stop in Berea to do some Christmas shopping in

the wonderful shops along Main Street. I ordered, among other things, personalized hand-knit Christmas stockings for everyone in my family from Warren's shop. As our family grew, so did our Christmas stocking collection, and we still hang them on the great-room mantel each year at Christmas.

Warren grew up as the youngest of ten children on a farm in Carroll County, Kentucky. His father and grandfather did woodworking and Warren, at a very young age, was encouraged to experiment in the family's workshop.

Warren and his energetic wife, Frankye, have worked hard over many years to bring Berea the recognition it well deserves for being a regional crafts center. In fact, they and the other many active craftspeople in Berea, especially those in the Kentucky Guild of Artists and Craftsmen, were instrumental in Berea's recently being officially designated the "Folk Arts and Crafts Capital of Kentucky."

Berea's Main Street wouldn't be the same without Warren's Upstairs Gallery and his storefront woodworking workshop just around the corner, where passersby can watch Warren and his assistants through the window making dulcimers and fine pieces of furniture

Warren has crafted over fifty-three hundred dulcimers, each signed, dated, numbered and registered. He uses basic woodworking skills and only native Kentucky woods to make his instruments. He has mastered over twenty different styles of dulcimers and they have appeared in Smithsonian shops and catalogs, in numerous magazines, and in private collections.

Each of Warren's furniture pieces is individually designed and handcrafted and made of wood Warren personally selects for its grain, color, and natural beauty.

Warren May is a multitalented craftsman, a dedicated civic leader and family man, and a truly delightful person to know.

A "Kentucky-style" piece of furniture has, first of all, an honesty of function. Just call it sound construction, but with simple, proud lines.

To design, visualize, and execute a good piece from start to finish is very difficult. I don't do nearly as well on paper as I do once I get to the wood; you can see that from my sketches. Once I get my piece of wood in hand and I pick up the grain pattern, I can see the proportions and feel really good about it. There's quite a bit to

making a piece of consequence — to make a piece that's clean and functional and that has a simple, classical stance — country classical.

Furniture making is greatly under-appreciated as a craft. People will walk into the shop down here and walk right by those three cherry pieces and you'll be just working up a storm and they'll say, "Well, we thought you'd be working on furniture." People are so saturated with store furniture that handmade furniture might have lost its impact as a craft. It's hard for people to visualize a piece until it's finished.

"I'm a woodworker. I use just really basic hand tools, and we don't use tape measures here."

I was trained in classical furniture construction, so designing and building a Queen Anne piece seems natural. However, even when I build a very casual piece of furniture or a Kentucky-style piece, I still use a classical approach to proportion and joinery.

I do my best work when I actually get a board in hand I can take a pile of seemingly common or uninteresting wood and create

39

a beautiful piece of furniture out of it. Since I quit doing commission work I've been able to create some more of my own designs.

We don't use tape measures here. It doesn't matter what size a board is; if it's not the right size, its not right. If I need to cut a board for a door or cabinet, I take the board and set it in the cabinet and make a mark on it. There's no fooling around and no guesswork. It's going to be on the mark.

My family migrated up through the Cumberland Gap, not far from here. I'm the youngest of ten kids — five boys and five girls. My dad would take the older boys and go out and do the farm work and I would putter around in the shop, trying to make bows and arrows. My dad could do anything in woodwork. Both my grandfathers made furniture. My grandmother was part Cherokee Indian. She could do straw weaving, one of the old Cherokee crafts.

Frankye and I chose to live in Berea. It has a sense of honesty about it. We quit teaching, drew out our retirement, drove down here in a Volkswagen and prayed a lot. Berea was becoming a crafts center and there were a lot of quality crafts here. We built our business very slowly and steadily.

There's a really high burn-out factor in a family crafts situation. I think if my wife hadn't been strong enough in her belief in me and in us as a family unit, we wouldn't have made it. She has really encouraged me. She could've gotten tired of all my nights in the woodshop and given up.

I really do think we have one of the more valuable, legitimate, optimistic craft businesses in Kentucky. Starting from scratch, too. We've done what we had to do.

A Queen Anne secretary bookcase. "These pieces of mine are interpretations. I try to get the feel of older pieces. Queen Anne is my real specialty."

"I like to take a piece of wood that has a beautiful grain in it and make an original design. I'm into artistic expression in the wood."

T e r r y   R a t l i f f

"It's all part of the dream," furniture maker Terry Ratliff tells us as his father's four-wheel-drive pickup truck inches its way up the steep side of the mountain to his home just outside Manton, Kentucky, near Prestonsburg. The dream began over seven years ago when Terry and his wife, Deborah, decided to forgo jobs as community mental-health workers to build their own log home in the mountains and to create completely independent lives for themselves and their children.

Terry and Deborah live in the heart of Appalachia with their two young children, Carlie and Joseph, right next door to Terry's eighty-four-year-old grandmother, Lizzie, who treated us to a private showing of her magnificent personal quilt collection. Terry's father, who migrated to Indiana for work when the coal mines closed at Manton, is now retired and lives just down the road from Terry.

In his home workshop, Terry carves beautiful tables and chairs, stools, and rocking horses, all out of trees he cuts down from the hills behind his house. He carves each piece from a single tree so it ages uniformly and — as is true of his house — his pieces contain no nails, screws, or glue.

Deborah, very pretty and very smart, is one of her husband's most ardent admirers. She perhaps best described his innate skills: "Terry sees things in wood. He doesn't take wood and put something together like a carpenter would. He doesn't work from blueprints. He creates from his mind, which is a talent that you're born with."

His pieces have been featured in magazines, exhibited in museums, galleries, and numerous crafts shows, and sold to people all over the country.

"Do you think you'll want to do this forever?" I ask him. "Just till I die," he says with a smile.

The day we visited, Terry's family had sent fresh fruit salad and homemade cherry pie up to the house to welcome us. At the big round kitchen table, on hickory-bark chairs made by Terry, we learned why these two college-educated young people savor their simple, sometimes harrowing, but always rewarding life in the eastern Kentucky mountains.

My interest in woodworking grew from an interest in log houses. I helped a friend build a hand-hewn house a while back. The work I did joining logs, building cabinets, and building furniture fed my interest.

I did cabinetry a while, mostly traditional styles, using boards instead of plywood. I made replicas of antique dry sinks and benches. From there my focus turned to furniture built entirely by hand tools, shaped from logs rather than lumber.

The bark-bottomed chairs I make are a big part of the heritage of eastern Kentucky because hill people have always taken advantage of what was available.

My methods have been termed "purist" because I cut down and split the trees myself, cure the wood, and strip the hickory bark that I use for seats and chair backs. What elevates my chairs from the ordinary, I believe, is the aesthetic quality that I strive for in each piece of furniture. It's an expression of feeling. It's not just a functional object. It's a statement and there are people to whom it says something.

I am a self-taught artisan. My work is a cross between traditional wood joinery and sculpture. The green-wood joinery process I use is a tradition identified with furniture making in the Southern hills.

The primary tools I use are the hewing hatchet, froe, drawknife, spokeshave, and shaving horse. I cut the trees during the winter months while the sap is down. I use wedges to split the log into bolts of wood. Splitting separates the wood fibers more closely to the grain pattern, not through the fibers, as sawing can. Chair parts are roughed out by splitting with a froe for more controlled splitting. The shaving horse and hewing hatchet are used to square up posts and chair rungs. Then each chair part is shaped using the shaving horse as a vise to hold the wood while it is hand carved with a drawknife and spokeshave. This hand work gives you a not-quite-round look and a handmade quality that you won't find in lathe-turned work.

The bark is stripped using the drawknife

"I use native hardwoods. The larger diameter trees are the best — something at least fourteen inches in diameter. The wood is more stable out of a larger tree."

while the sap is up between April and July, just as they did in the past. The bark is rolled up and stored until I need it. We soak the bark to make it pliable again so that we can weave seats all year round.

The character of these pieces is also helped by the care we give the finishes. Hand-rubbed oil finishes allow the grain to be appreciated and enjoyed by the eye as well as the touch.

I use only hardwoods native to this region. I get my trees from people I know. Sometimes I get trees ahead of strip miners' bulldozers. I want my work to be a tribute to the spirit of producing beauty and func-

tion from resources readily available.

Making chairs is a nice way to make a living. I do it for what it feels like when it is all done. I love the freedom, the independence, the confidence it gives me. Five or six days a week we are living our dream and we are lucky people to do it. There are a few days a week when we think this is a bunch of bunk and we probably ought to be doing something else, or there ought to be an easier way to make a living. But then I deliver chairs to some lawyer or some company president in a big, cold office, and I realize he would like to be right here. This is his fantasy.

"People like the story behind my pieces. That's real important to them. You can feel it. It's something almost alive, something that has a soul. Something that I've put something into . . . a creation."

LEFT: "The first high chair I ever made." OPPOSITE: "That's Carlie on Roman Beauty. He's an Appaloosa horse who came out of an apple tree."

Jim Massey

From behind the small house in Fisherville, Kentucky, we could hear the sound of wood mallet meeting chisel, and I knew we had found Jim Massey. There, in his workshop, Jim was hand-shaping the flank of one of his trademark items — a wooden horse. This particular horse was a three-foot-high sculpture, carved in great detail and left unsanded so that the intricate cut-marks could be seen.

I was lucky enough in 1981 to buy one of the first rocking horses Jim ever made. It sits in its place of honor in my den at Cave Hill Place. Both my children, Lincoln and Pamela, have enjoyed rocking and playing on it, and now that they're older, I get to enjoy it as a piece of art. I have since purchased another horse which sits on the

hearth in the dining room — truly a work of art, not to be ridden by small children.

Jim is an art school-trained Louisvillian who can do many things in wood, from carpentry to cabinetmaking to furniture to art. But his reputation was established by making beautiful rocking horses, and that is what currently takes up most of his time. The horses have become a long-running study for Jim, who researches the details of horse conformation, but chooses not to make his horses literally lifelike. As he explained, "I started out making two-dimensional, simplified cutouts; then a cartoony-looking thing; then a more anatomically correct form, even though it didn't really match a real horse bone-for-bone. But I think they're starting to express more of what I had in mind, and they're certainly more lifelike than most hobby horses I've seen."

Jim is the first of Kentucky's craftspeople to tell me how the Vietnam war played a part in shaping his creative life. Like other veterans, Jim was profoundly affected by his experience in Vietnam. The war prompted

his decision to pursue life as an artist on his return to the States. The decision changed his life for the better, he believes, as do the many Kentuckians who now admire and collect his work.

After going to Vietnam, I finally decided to listen to myself and have a little confidence to just do it. All this stuff people tell you about doing what you want — I found out it's true. All you have to do is pay your dues, do it. Whatever you decide to do, you can do it. There were times when I almost gave up on art completely. People told me it was foolish, that I was wasting my time, that artists' lives were always tragic. But Vietnam was the catalyst that said, "Look, you could be gone from this world tomorrow, and you haven't done a damn thing you want to do." So when I got back, things changed. I looked at the world differently. Once you see the aesthetics of the universe, once you see

Jim, outside his shop, with one of his signature crafts, a rocking horse.

things as an artist, you can't quit. Once you see things that way, you can't see them any other way.

I've always dedicated my life to the aesthetics of the world. So when I finally realized there was a business side to this thing, I started selling pieces at art shows and fairs. I eventually got, through word of mouth, some cabinet work and furniture work. That kept evolving until I became sort of a wholesale supplier to shops and galleries. That got to be too much, and now, when I finish a piece, it's for sale. There are no restrictions on me to make a piece like yesterday's piece, although I will do a commission once in a while. The buyers come and look around and pick out what they want.

I stumbled onto the horses, actually. I was looking for something I could be challenged by on a daily basis, but that was saleable. I played around with some horse ideas — rocking horses and so on. I took some children's rockers to the first show we went to, and I think we sold five of them. People got excited about them, and I did, too. I had found a subject I could refine.

Eighty percent of the people who buy my things are collectors or decorators. They see my horses as objects, not toys. I make a small rocker that doesn't have as much mane, and is directed more towards the child's hobby horse. Kids ride those, but most of them are sculptural and are looked at as objects.

I really don't keep track, but it takes me about a hundred hours to make a horse. It goes so fast. You find one little thing wrong and you start working on it, and before you know it, it's one o'clock in the morning. I find myself saying, at midnight, "I'll be up in a minute, honey!"

Wood works with you and you work with it after a while. It will resist in ways that tell you you're doing something wrong, that maybe you should rethink your design or approach it a different way. Eventually the wood will show you how to do it. It's not like metal with no grain, where you can start in any direction you want to.

I don't really care about whether my stuff is art or craft. As far as the universe is concerned, I'm an artist. As far as my vocation goes, I feel that I'm a craftsman. Call it whatever you want, it's all right by me. As long as I can work and I'm pleased with the work, as long as I can earn a living wage, you can call it anything you want.

R u d e   O s o l n i k

Rude Osolnik is a master wood turner from Berea, Kentucky. Rude has dedicated his life to the perfection of his own skills as a wood turner and to passing those skills on to the hundreds of fortunate students he has taught over the forty years he has headed the department of industrial arts at Berea College in Berea, Kentucky.

Rude told us when we visited one afternoon, "You've got to share your talents. You can't just keep them. What you share with others always comes back to you."

Since retiring in 1978, Rude has continued to conduct numerous seminars, lectures, and demonstrations around the country. It says something about Rude that when asked what he would do with a million dollars if it were given to him, he replied that he would set up scholarships at Berea College. In fact, he has already established a thousand-dollar scholarship at Berea in his wife, Daphne's, memory.

Daphne, Rude will tell you, was the one who "held it all together" for him until she passed away a few months before we visited. While he taught all day, Daphne would meticulously oil, seal, and hand finish the pieces he had completed the night before. They worked closely and creatively together and instilled a love for their artistry in their children, especially their son, Joe, who runs a crafts shop in Berea.

Rude is held in high esteem by wood turners around the country for the beautiful pieces he chisels from solid blocks of exotic, aged woods. He seeks out unique woods with unusual markings and grains

and converts them into works of art. One of his bowls is in the permanent collection at the Smithsonian Museum.

Rude has also designed and patented several woodturning tools which are sold nationally through woodturning publications. He made all the tools he uses now in his work.

Rude proudly showed us the stacks of wood he has collected over the years, of all types and sizes. We asked him what he was going to do with all that wood and he said, "It's eventually going to be something."

Rude presented me with a small bud vase that he turned while I was there. It was made of exotic bacote wood and inspired by Egyptian ceramics.

When I asked him if he thought he was one of the master wood turners of the world, he said, "I don't know. They say I am. I guess I have been doing this long enough to say so. But I just enjoy doing it."

There is something magical about Rude's ability to take a rough piece of wood and "turn" it into a beautiful work of art.

It all started in 1927. I had a teacher that was Swiss. His father had a furniture shop over in Switzerland, and he taught me industrial arts, what used to be called "manual training." And the thing that I appreciated most from him was that he made me very conscious of design. A piece had to look pretty. It had to have the right proportions and you had to use interesting wood.

People think I work with just unusual woods, but that's not so. Some of our native woods are fairly exotic, especially the ones that have been through an aging, decaying process. You have to take wood at the right time and then put it up where it will dry. That keeps the fungus from working on it. All the discoloration you see on my pieces actually is fungus that has gotten into the wood.

Sometimes when I get a piece of wood I leave it sitting around maybe for four or five months while I look at it, and then all of a sudden it will hit me what to do with it. Sometimes you look at a piece and the size of it, the way it is fashioned out, pretty well determines what the object will be. You try to visualize what it will become and, actually, it is like having a mental picture of what that piece is going to look like.

In the early days, most of my turnings

"Turning wood is taking a raw piece of wood and, in a matter of a half hour, having something tangible and beautiful to show."

were basically utilitarian pieces. But a piece not only has to be functional, it should be attractive.

A wood turner is the reverse of a potter. The potter takes a piece of clay and moves it around to form an object. A wood turner takes a piece of wood and removes the wood in the right places to create shapes.

Each piece of wood is like a human fingerprint. No two pieces are alike. It's funny how wood turners get to the point where they see stumps and think bowls.

RIGHT: "I designed these candle holders back in the early 1950s and the more I worked on them, the more I found those slender, graceful lines. I put five kids through school selling those things."

B r i a n   B o g g s

The special pride Brian Boggs takes in the craft of chair making is best evidenced by the last line in his brochure: "All my work is guaranteed to last my lifetime."

Brian Boggs is an example of the spirit motivating the best of Kentucky's craftspeople who choose to forgo steady jobs and easy lives in order to pursue perfection of a craft. In Brian's case, he has chosen to support his wife and two young children on the money he earns hand making chairs in Berea, Kentucky.

He also designs and makes many of the tools he uses to make his chairs.

Brian's family is obviously supportive of

his business. His wife is his business partner and most trusted adviser on chair designs and quality. His young sons often help him split logs and smooth and shape wood pieces. You often see Brian's family with him at crafts shows and demonstrations here in Kentucky. His devotion to his work, his family, and to his simple but happy way of life is enviable. To me he is the personification of the true Appalachian spirit in Kentucky.

I build my chairs the old way. All posts, rungs, and slats are rived from choice logs to ensure trueness to the grain. A joiner and band saw help out with the rough work, but the shaping and smoothing are done with a drawknife and a spokeshave. All joinery is cut by hand. I put super dry rungs into moist posts so the chair tightens as the posts dry. Slats, rockers, and arms are pinned into place. Glue provides additional insurance. I work with oak, ash, hickory, and maple. Seats are woven from hickory bark or oak splints, which I make myself. I stuff wood shavings between the layers of the seat for added

comfort and extended wear. As much as I can, I stick with my hand tools. I would rather make chairs as a hobby and do something else for a living than have to use machine tools.

I'm sticking to chairs. I tried a couple of different tables, but I've found them too impractical. I don't enjoy it anyway. I like chairs. My chairs are good sturdy chairs — they're Appalachian. They're nice and light. They're real good for around a table. I make about forty-five different styles of chairs.

I like sitting in my chairs. They're very comfortable. I'd like to own some, but it doesn't bother me that much that we don't. The kids have their own chairs, and we have the first one I ever made. I made a stool for my wife last year because she threatened to go out and buy the ugliest chairs in the world if I didn't make something for us. So I made a stool and that calmed her down a little bit. I just can't afford to take the time to build something for us.

I love designing. I design a lot more than I can afford to build. I've got pages and pages of designs that I've done — just sketchy things — that I haven't been able

to produce because I don't have the time to develop the process for doing the design. I think I could enjoy doing that if I wouldn't have to change my life-style. If I had to move to a big city to do this, I don't think I'd do it. It's just hard for me to imagine doing anything else right now because I like chair making so much.

I just want to be able to enjoy working on a chair without pressure from the need for money. I don't think money is important to very many craftsmen. I never had any. If it was very important to me, I'd be in sad shape. My goal is not to be famous. My goal is to become a true master at what I do. And I'm a long way off. It takes a lot of time.

"I hardly ever use regular tools. Most of the ones I use I've designed and made. With the help of a machinist, I even invented a machine that will split bark. All of my spoke shanks, I've either made or taken the basic style from something commercial and blown everything away but for one point and built around it."

"I don't think making hand-made things is going to die out, because the more people live high-tech life-styles, the more important it is for them to have something around them that is homemade, something of interest. Something they can have a warm feeling about, a story about. Not a factory-made object. I think we'll be around a while."

R o n   I s a a c s

Ron Isaacs will tell you he is not a Kentucky craftsman at all. He is an artist who, in the course of creating his art, uses wood to achieve some remarkable effects. The manipulation of the wood is more than incidental to the work, however, and for that reason Ron could call himself a craftsman if he wanted to. No matter what label you put on him, the trompe l'oeil masterpieces he creates are stunning examples of an artist in control of both his materials and his color.

Judging from major gallery and collector recognition in New York, I would say that Ron is one of Kentucky's best-known artists. His creations command fees commensurate with his stature in the art world, and it is easy to see why. His pieces are humorous — the very idea of trompe l'oeil implies a

desire to amuse — but they are serious art.

Ron keeps a sketchbook full of elaborate doodles which often transform into designs for his next creation. At other times, he just starts working with objects, clothing, and other materials until something clicks. Regardless of what inspires him, his extraordinary sculptural still lifes always bring rave reviews from critics and viewers alike.

There's a lot of silliness involved in a grown man's making plywood lingerie. I think we all impose a little silliness on ourselves in the name of art. But there's something kind of whimsical about that, too. It's kind of fun to take something soft, like clothing or cloth, and make it out of a hard material. Yet, somehow, the two look almost identical, which leads us to question the nature of reality. Reality is just whatever you're inclined to think it is. So, I have a little fun with what I do.

The trompe l'oeil aspects of my work

— the "fool the eye" aspects — are not for me the primary goal. It's a kind of thing that's a lot of fun to play with — and the human eye is easily deceived — but it's more because I want to use these objects and these images. Building with plywood and paint is one way to arrive at that. So I would say that it's not an end in itself, it's a means toward an end, especially recently, as I'm making images that have more resonance psychologically, as well as visually. The primary reasons why I choose objects to reproduce in plywood and paint are formal reasons. I like the way something's shaped or I like its structure or its color or its texture or its pattern, and how it might be combined with other shapes in some sort of a lyrical way with some sort of visual interest.

I think I choose certain objects for reasons I don't fully understand. There is an intuitive psychological level that I respond to. I like open-ended content, both for the viewer and for myself, too. I like the fact that I can look back at pieces and find connotations and associations that I didn't even see while I was making them. I like the viewer to have that opportunity, too. I know to an extent that it's hard to verbalize, and, as I say, I'm primarily working with a visual vocabulary rather than a verbal vocabulary, anyway. I like to leave it at that.

For trompe l'oeil imagery, I will pin up the object, say a garment or leaves or whatever, to a gridded-off piece of paper of one-inch squares on Styrofoam board. And from that I will make a contour-line drawing on another piece of paper with one-inch squares so that I can see where the edge crosses through certain squares and you can get an exact size. Then I can do the interior lines. From that I start making tracing-paper patterns, analyzing the form into planes of wood. Sometimes it takes as many as six hundred pieces of wood to build an elaborate or large piece. The wood is sawed out on a scroll saw and a jigsaw. About the only tools I use are the scroll saw and a belt and disk sander. I use Elmer's carpenter glue to glue the pieces together. I do a little sanding on it. A little bit of plastic wood just for minor transitions, not for major construction or anything. I'm sort of a purist in that respect. Add a couple of coats of Liquitex, sand it again and it's ready to paint. So at that point I've reached a stage that most artists do when they've primed a canvas and they're ready to paint on it. But that's actually about half my work. It depends on the piece. Some are difficult to construct, and others are difficult to paint.

I like all sorts of things. I like some things that are extremely primitive-looking, very crudely done with a kind of expressionistic urgency, and other things that are very technically refined. Strangely enough, I think a lot of technically refined things are

often very uninteresting, because I guess I know how easy technique is, and what a common commodity it is in the art world. There are hundreds of thousands of artists out there who are technically skilled who haven't had an idea in years.

My work is getting more sculptural, more

"My pieces aren't carved, they're constructed. They're just lots of pieces of shaped wood."

three-dimensional. I don't have immediate plans to leave working with wood. I enjoy it a great deal.

"I had to, more or less, invent sculpture for myself. I came to it through the back door. In 1970, I sawed out a piece of plywood, put an image on it, and mounted it on a canvas to raise it off the surface and add interest to the imagery."

 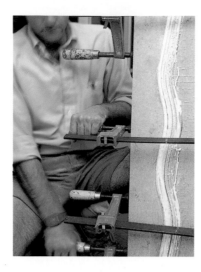 

L y n n   S w e e t

Lynn Sweet was born near Detroit in the fifties, so it is no surprise that his signature piece is a mahogany desk that he hand carved in the shape of a 1957 Chevrolet Bel Air dashboard. The dash and the hood piece which inspired the desk's leg panels still hang from the ceiling of Lynn's design studio at the University of Kentucky in Lexington.

To meet Lynn at the university, conservatively dressed in his oxford-cloth shirt and khakis, one would never suspect that this mild-mannered teacher-artist could create the wild and whimsical pieces for which he is now so well known.

Lynn teaches woodworking there and supervises the wood shop while he experiments with his latest self-styled "Art Wack-

O" furniture designs. Lynn's extraordinary flair for design and manipulation of unusual materials have earned him great respect and accolades in the finest arts-and-crafts circles in this region.

At age 37, Lynn puts "everything I've learned over the last seventeen years into everything I make." His pieces are sophisticated works of art with an urban appeal, but his heart is squarely rooted in Kentucky. Lynn's family still lives near him outside Lexington, and he spends much of his spare time racing bicycles across the Kentucky countryside.

I've always drawn and I still enjoy drawing, but I'm more a sculptor than a painter. Furniture making isn't sculpture in the traditional sense, but my furniture is not traditional and it certainly includes elements of both painting and sculpture. A lot of my works now are painted. As a kid I started drawing things — horses, cars, buildings, people — and that was my

idea of what an artist does. Then I started making furniture. After working for several years with a man who taught me to make furniture, I got a job with the Kentucky Historical Society, actually with the restoration of the old State Capitol in 1973. I stayed at the Historical Society for another six or seven years as the museum technician, and during that time I continued to make reproductions of antiques. However, I started kind of bending the edges and working with different ideas and compiling original-design furniture, largely with the lines of other antique precedents. My first truly original-design piece was the Phelps chair, the tall blond chair. I made six of those in exchange for an old sports car, a very nice old sports car. That chair had a lot of Art Nouveau influences. I was reading books on the movement, and the ideas and forms appealed to me. But I was still working inside the grammar of antiques. You could still see that it looked a lot like a Queen Anne chair.

The work I was doing then had a lot to

do with reverence for wood and letting the beauty of the wood be a big part of the piece. Now, I'm denying all that. I'm making things look like they are plastic or steel or leather or marble and I'm denying the appearance of traditional woodworking. I still use mortise-and-tenon joints and still use dovetail joints on drawers. I still use traditional woodworking. You can't see it from the outside. It's a trick.

Wood is still the best material for me because it's what I really feel very confident in. For me, wood is the most plastic of the materials that I could work with just because I have experience behind me. I have a good idea what tools I need. I know where the envelope stops. Wood has the ability to twist or bend or be laminated. I'm incorporating stone, plastic, steel, other materials in my work and I intend to continue doing that. Materials and processes are what fascinate me. I want to incorporate them all eventually.

The function of my furniture becomes incidental. It's a table, and you still can put a vase of flowers or a lamp or throw your keys on it when you come in the door, but that's not the point. The point is, it's an object. You look at it and take in this point, this form, this color. It's more for looking at, to make you think. Right now, with a lot of these pieces that I'm working on, "tableness" becomes secondary to the "objectness" of it. Ornamentalism is what a lot of this is also about.

I like the cerebral end of designing very much. I enjoy looking through art books and architecture books and grabbing an idea here and having a thought there and coming back and putting two and two together. I guess I've always kind of hoped that I would find myself just designing someday — just coming up with a design, making the prototype, then going on to the next design. These things I'm making now

really are prototypes. However, I wouldn't want you to think that I don't enjoy going out and getting sawdust in my hair and working with these materials. I really love it. I can't imagine stopping.

I certainly enjoy finishing a piece, signing it, putting it down, and looking at it for an hour or so. While I'm sitting there looking at it, I'm thinking, well, I love the way this element works. How can I incorporate that in the next piece or a similar piece without just making another of the same piece? I also look at it and I say, well, I don't like that about this piece. How can I avoid ever finding myself in this position again? I

"If you see wood in a piece of mine now, it's an exotic wood, meant to dazzle and amuse. But underneath it I'm using maple and poplar, hardwoods from Kentucky."

don't think I've ever made anything that was perfect. Something is always just shy of perfect for me. There's tension there. It pushes me. I'm always anxious to make another piece — to dive into another one to see if I can make the form pop for me, make a new idea really work. I love knowing a piece is done, knowing I did it, seeing it finished. I love doing this work.

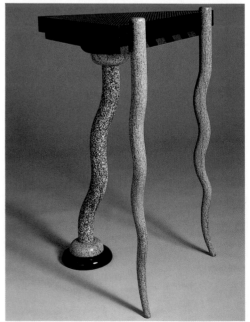

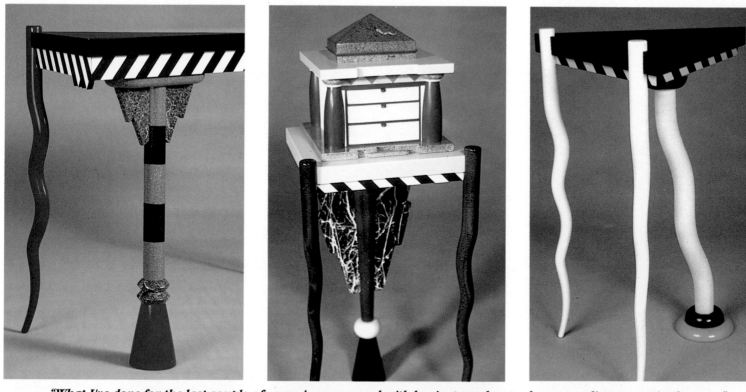

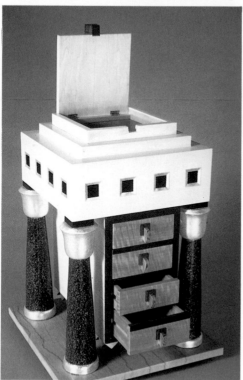

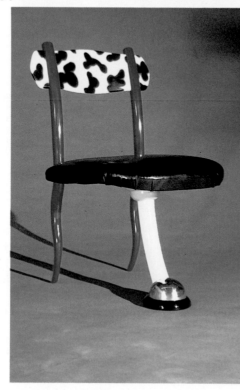

"What I've done for the last couple of years is cover wood with laminate and water-borne acrylic automotive lacquer."

Textiles and Quilts

Churchill Weavers

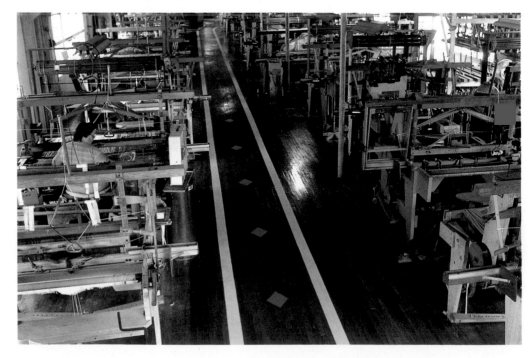

The public gallery at Churchill Weavers houses one of Kentucky's most interesting displays of crafts. But a trip to Churchill Weavers in Berea, Kentucky, is not complete without a tour of its loom house, where some of the world's most beautiful baby blankets, throws, shawls, ties, and other handwoven goods are made.

Visitors from all over the world have made pilgrimages to Berea to see Churchill Weavers' famous seventy-year-old hand-built looms and to admire the creative skills of the talented craftspeople who have worked there for decades.

My friends, current owners Lila and Richard Bellando, work together to continue the hand-weaving legacy of Churchill Weavers.

Their beautiful daughter, Tara, who has been screen-tested in Hollywood and worked with an agency for rock bands in New York, was just coming home the day we visited — to weave again for her family's business.

The Bellandos were hand-picked by the original owners to carry on the business and they consider it a trust. Those of us who admire their work are grateful that they have chosen to continue the legacy.

We "inherited" Churchill Weavers from some remarkable people— Mr. Carroll Churchill and his wife, Eleanor. They met in India when Mr. Churchill, an industrial engineer at Westinghouse, was sent on a foreign mission to invent faster, more efficient looms for the Indian caste weavers. After he completed his project, the Churchills moved to Berea — supposedly to develop a Department of Physics and Mechanics at Berea College, but it never materialized. Instead, they took advantage of a unique opportunity to expand Berea's budding hand-weaving craft industry and to help create much-needed jobs in the region.

Mr. Churchill designed and built brand new fly-shuttle looms and opened Churchill Weavers in 1922. The Churchills survived many lean years, and eventually developed Churchill Weavers into a thriving business.

In 1972, Mrs. Churchill approached us to buy Churchill Weavers. We were astonished and overwhelmed at the thought of such a huge undertaking.

Mrs. Churchill told us that she specifically chose us to be the next owners. She had been watching us, and felt that we would try hard to keep Churchill Weavers alive and well as a business. She also felt that we would be concerned about the employees and that we would keep their life's work ongoing. After several sleepless weeks, we decided to burn all our bridges and do it, and it has been a very rewarding and wonderful thing for us.

We keep our loom house open so that people can come through and see the work being done. Many people are made aware of hand weaving who were not actually aware of it before. Although some people come here because of the weaving, others don't expect it and are amazed to see how the fabric is woven and how many times it is touched by people who care about it.

They are surprised to see how the process begins in the warp, how the warp is put into the looms and how it is actually woven into fabric. We feel that by having fly-shuttle looms, we have been able to offer hand woven goods at a more reasonable price; therefore, they have been made available to more people.

Another thing we are proud to be doing is teaching other hand weavers something about operating a crafts business that can support itself. Lots of weavers write to us, or they come here and ask questions. They want to know how they can make the business part of it work. We always try to find time to sit down and work with people, telling them as much as we know about it.

We feel we have become an institution in a way. People recognize our name and associate it with quality and tradition — something they can depend on — and that means a lot to us.

Over the years Churchill Weavers has employed untold numbers of people — we couldn't even begin to know how many people have worked here in the almost seventy years that this company has been in business. But it's a nice thing to meet someone and they say to you, "Oh, yes, Churchill Weavers, my mother used to work there," or, "My grandmother used to work there." We think we've made some impact on the community's economics by providing employment, and we think the community is proud to have us here. People drive many miles to see us. We schedule quite a few guided tours through the loom house — school groups, bus tours, college classes in home economics, fashion design, marketing, and so on.

We feel we have an obligation to remember our heritage, so we do use some traditional coverlet patterns. We keep those in the line because they are good. We feel a strong tie to tradition; on the other hand,

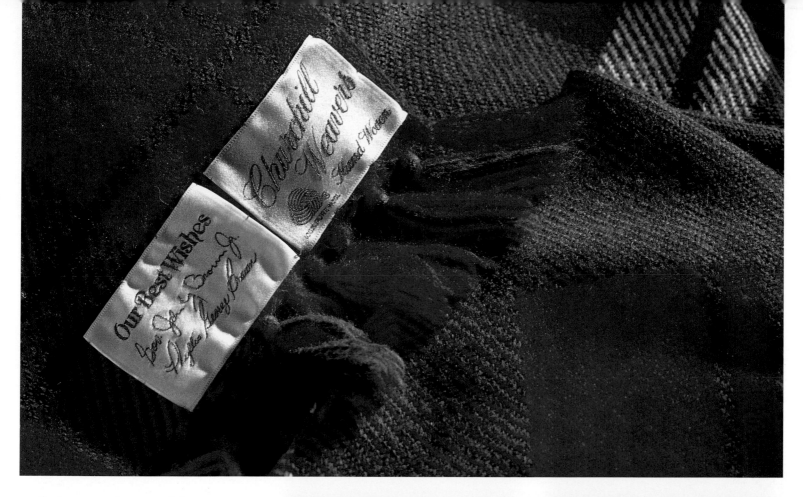

we feel very much a part of the contemporary world. We take today's colors and weave them together in beautifully textured products, and we use traditional methods to do it.

We love the spirit of this place, love the feeling that's here. We like seeing a new design when it first comes off the loom. After we've been through the "idea" part, been through the "designing session," and we see the warp made, we begin to get excited. And then, when we see the first woven fabric and know that it worked, that's wonderfully exciting.

We think the way to describe Churchill Weavers' "hallmark of excellence" is integrity. We try for honestly beautiful designs and we stand behind our product and our word. We feel that way about the crafts we produce and about our business.

Quicksand Crafts

The eastern Kentucky mountains have been the wellspring for a great many of our state's native craftspeople. The traits that a hard mountain life build — stamina, individuality, self-reliance — are traits that make good artisans. "Mountain crafts" have become almost a category of artwork unto themselves. Nestled in those mountains among the hollows of Knott County is one of the most creative and successful weaving operations in Kentucky — the Quicksand Crafts Center at Vest, Kentucky.

I drove from Prestonsburg one morning deep into the breathtaking and mysterious hills and hollows of Appalachia to find Vest — a tiny community of 120 families — comprised mostly of two main buildings, the Sutton General Store and a large old school building on the hill above it which houses Quicksand Crafts.

Quicksand Crafts is an extended community working together to weave rugs, placemats, and beautiful wall hangings. The Crafts Center provides weavers with much-needed income, but also fosters among them a tradition of excellence; a source of community pride; a meeting place where teaching and learning weaving skills among generations enhances the lives of everyone.

The inspiration for this community of artisans came from a remarkable woman, Naoma Powell, who after years of teaching art at the University of Toledo, Ohio, felt the call in the 1960s to do something more with her life and accepted a job with the Hindman Settlement School to teach art to the children of Appalachia. Naoma's commit-

ment to these children began with her introducing them to the beauty and wonders of their environment, and fostering within them a sense of pride and identification with the generations of Appalachians who came before them. She slowly introduced art, music, reading, and other culturally enriching experiences into their lives; and, when she saw the zeal with which they responded, she grew increasingly committed to a brighter future for the children — to breaking the chain of poverty many of these children's families were caught within after the closing of the coal mines in the area.

Naoma's work led to the establishment of a cottage crafts industry, so the women of Quicksand Creek could weave saleable items right in their homes while tending to household chores and raising children, and the men could do woodworking and pottery and various other crafts while the mines were closed. The Crafts Center became the outlet for marketing the textiles and other crafts being produced in people's homes. Naoma, the programs she started, and the

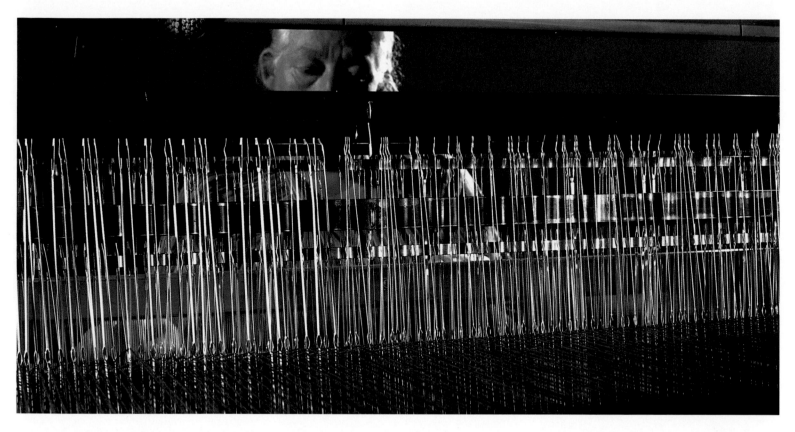

government-grant programs she lured, provided training, materials, and much-needed marketing assistance, and the area prospered from its newly developed talents.

Naoma Powell now teaches art at the University of Missouri. She is modest about her accomplishments. It is the people of Kentucky, she says, who deserve the credit: "Quicksand Crafts grew slowly and solidly because many believed in the potential of the people, who needed only encouragement to become the excellent craftsmen they are today, through their own persistence, and joy in working."

When Naoma left, the reins were passed to another extraordinary woman — Arkie Patton — one of the Crafts Center's finest weavers before she chose to forgo a successful dry-cleaning business to take over the directorship of the Crafts Center. Arkie's business professionalism, her high stan-

dards for product quality, her excellent training skills, and keen eye for the center's future are largely responsible for its becoming the commercially successful and admired Appalachian crafts source it is today.

When we visited Vest, we toured the center with Arkie, and discovered that day what motivated her to dedicate her life to this worthwhile program.

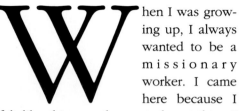

hen I was growing up, I always wanted to be a missionary worker. I came here because I felt like this was the next closest thing I could do to help people — to bring them in and to train them to weave, to provide a way for them to work and be with people. I felt like I was helping people more by

doing this. I always say, if somebody can count to ten and if they're interested in weaving, I can teach that person to weave.

I was on the board of directors of the Center for several years before I became a director. I knew Naoma when she was at Quicksand, and I just became very interested in what she was doing and I looked her up.

There was nothing for women around here to do then — no recreation, no kind of employment. They had no outlet, really. They raised babies and they canned food. They did their best. They made quilts for their own use but not for sale. Back then, there wasn't any coal-mine work. There was a recession. The biggest portion of the people around here didn't have education enough to make it away from here. The people who were in business moved out. But the people that came up didn't have the

education to feel confident that they could go out and make it in the world. The unfortunate thing is that there are an awful lot of bright young people from here, and the ones that do manage to get an education don't have any opportunities, so they leave. So it just leaves the people who don't have the chance or don't want the opportunity, and they just stay because they have no place to go. The young generation has to have something to occupy them or to get them started in something.

At the time I became director, the weavers were doing lots of weaving. They owned their homes and their own looms. We would pick up the thread and bring it in, yards and yards of it. But there would be mistakes, and some of the women burned coal in their homes, so their things would be black and dirty and you couldn't sell them. There was a lot of stuff being done with good intentions, but it wasn't smart, businesswise. Now I think our business has taken a whole different turn. It has stopped being a cottage industry for individual women, and it's become a business. We hire the same people, but now they mostly work at our place. Once they are through our training program, they can weave and they also can take care of customers, give people tours of the building, and do anything that needs to be done here.

What we did was a timely thing. We had men out of work, families on welfare, women with talents but no outlets for those talents. Quicksand made it all work.

J o y c e   J u s t u s

Walk into the stately three-story home of Joyce Justus in historic Middletown, Kentucky, and you enter a life-size "doll house" — home to soft-sculpture dolls and the talented craftswoman who has made them famous. Joyce has combined lifelong professional sewing skills with her finely trained landscape-painter's eye to create what can best be described as "three-dimensional Norman Rockwells."

Joyce sculpts one-of-a-kind dolls, many in settings depicting life situations recog-nizable to us all — a wife turned insomniac by the loud snoring of her bed partner; a grandmother who has fallen asleep rocking a wide-awake baby. Her dolls tell sweet stories of simple human events and feelings. One can't help identifying with them.

The facial expressions she painstakingly creates with her needlework portray the subtlest of emotions. No detail is too fine, no accessory too intricate for this quiet perfectionist who will often redo her figures two and three times if they do not meet her high standards. Joyce is a gifted, sensitive craftswoman, whose dolls have been exhibited at the Smithsonian's Renwick Gallery and in craft galleries across the country.

I come from a family of women who liked to sew and do needle-work. I learned from them that I could take a needle and thread and make magic with it. Years ago I started realizing there was a lot of appreciation for needlework here in Kentucky, so I began doing more of it, which naturally led to the kind of needle sculpture I do now. Needle sculpture is an old medium. In the seventies there was a revival of interest in it and I felt for the first time I would like to try it. I became fascinated and amazed at how well the medium could be manipulated.

I've had artist friends take exception to the fact that I call what I do "doll making." They think it's a mistake, because they feel it puts me into the "craft" category instead of the "art" category. But some of the things I do are more doll-like than anything else.

My figures make statements about people and how they relate to each other. I try to actually create a three-dimensional personality portrait of a person. On the surface you may be able to say, "Oh, that's very doll-like," but, hopefully, if I have succeeded with that doll, I've conveyed more personality than a doll usually expresses.

I consider my work a blend of art and craft. There definitely is the craft end of it — the work and the stitching has to be there, the good construction technique. I

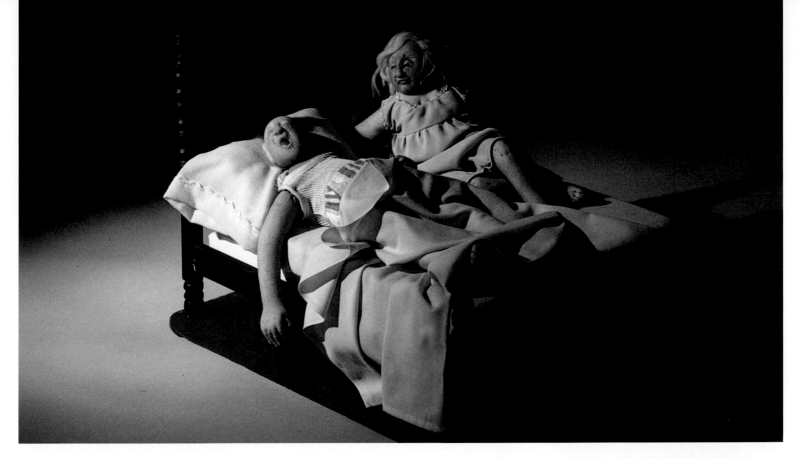

like the things I am making in this craft medium, but I am using it as an artist.

I have a background as a painter. I can draw but very seldom do anything elaborate. I do a figure drawing to scale and then I compare what I create with the figure drawing to keep things in proper proportion as I work. Unless a customer is specifically asking for an idea to be sketched out, I don't flesh out a full idea on paper. I do it all in my head. I will start thinking about the clothing that I want to put on the doll, the mood I want to create, the colors I want to use to do that. Then I start searching through fabrics or go to fabric stores to find just the right things. I pay a lot of attention to colors when I'm doing a piece, because I think the colors convey a lot of the message that I want to get across.

I don't think I am especially good at getting likenesses. I have tried it for people, and I've always felt that what I ended up with was more a caricature than a portrait.

I find it very difficult to capture exact likenesses in a fabric medium. I probably could if I were working in clay, but it's just not my thing. Getting all the creases in the face — the frowns and lines, the facial details — that's all needlework. The face is basically a ball, fiber-filled and covered with hosiery that sits down on the body. Then you actually sculpt — there's no better way to describe it — with needle and thread.

I don't think about a Joyce Justus style when I'm working. But I'm told there is a very definite style or look to my pieces. Someone can walk into a room with a number of needle-sculptured pieces and know immediately which ones I have done.

Sometimes I get ideas from books. For example, Charles Dickens was taken from photographs in books. Ideas come from all sorts of places. Sometimes a particular type of face will inspire me. I accumulate photos from everywhere — people with various

"I make dolls about things I care about — mainly family. Many of my dolls resemble my mother, because she has been an inspiration to me. But it's funny — the older I get the more they look like me, too."

expressions. I incorporate them into my work. The "Grandmother Rocking the Baby" is probably my favorite piece. She's gone to sleep and the baby, of course, is wide awake. It is one of a number of dolls I have made called "Contemporary People."

I live with my dolls because I am pleased with them and proud of them. After a while, they take on a life of their own. I don't even like to keep them under glass because I don't like to see them boxed in. If a doll is really successful, it should seem alive when you walk by it. All my dolls become a part of me when I finish them. If they sit around my house too long, I can't sell them. I find I have become too attached to them.

Nellie Charlton

"A nice visit really feeds your soul," says Nellie Charlton. We're sitting and chatting on her living-room couch, covered, of course, with one of her favorite nap quilts. Nellie is a traditional Kentucky quilter whose fine, detailed quilting of a Lone Star won her the blue ribbon in the quilting competition at the 1981 State Fair.

There is no better way to spend an afternoon than to share a nice visit with Nellie. She loves life, has many friends, and is devoted to her family, church, and community. She's been sewing all her life and quilting for over forty years. She quilts because she loves it, and her most recent quilts have been true labors of love — one, a quilting-group collaboration donated to her

local fire department for a fund-raising auction; another, a pictorial-appliqué quilt presented by Nellie to her church to commemorate its 125th anniversary.

Being such a quilt lover and collector, I relished every minute of my visit with Nellie in her cozy, immaculately kept home, especially when she pulled out her quilts.

The quilt trunk in her bedroom is a smorgasbord of every color and quilt design imaginable. Many of her quilts hold precious memories for her, of contests won and of happy collaborations with her artistic daughter, Mary, before she tragically died of cancer at age thirty-nine.

At seventy-seven, Nellie not only quilts but she also gardens, cuts her own grass, cleans her own house, and is an active volunteer; she is a self-proclaimed "contented spirit" who is an inspiration to us all.

She shared a tip with me the day I visited, and I'll pass it on to you — Keep your quilts folded up in pillowcases, never in plastic bags, so they can "breathe." All my quilts are now in pillowcases, too.

Traditional quilting is the only kind that interests me. I don't think I'm qualified to do it any other way. Not contemporary. I think for the most part people like the old styles, but maybe that will change over time. I don't know. The experience I've had, though, is that most people like quilts made the old-fashioned way.

I think the craft of quilting more or less started with the mountain people. They were not artists, you know, but they had artistic ability. They made them for utilitarian purposes. My mother had six girls and she made quilts to keep us warm. She made them out of the good parts of old clothing, out of the scraps she had left over from sewing. That's the way quilting started.

Quilting has always been a form of socializing. People called them quilting bees, you know. The neighbors would get together and talk and quilt. They could do a quilt in a few days that way. It takes me months! We have a quilting group out here

now that some of the women got together and started. We've been functioning for about four years, and we get together once a month to compare quilts and swap ideas and visit and just have a nice time. We have even worked on quilts together. We decided we'd make one as a group project. After we got it all fitted, it was really pretty. We gave it to the fire department at Shepherdsville and they auctioned it off and made a thousand dollars on it. We were real proud of ourselves for that. The poor firemen need help.

You can quilt on a machine, but I've never done one that way. I don't plan to. There are new techniques being developed all the time because there are so many more people quilting. There are also new supplies that help. But I won't use them because I'm not in any hurry. Quilting is just something I like to do. I think quilters my age have the same feeling about it. They do it because it's something they enjoy. Isn't that a good enough reason?

I collect quilts, and I know a lot about technique, but that doesn't interest me. I do the labor. I just stay right here and quilt. I'm seventy-seven years old. I do everything for myself. What I know about quilting I feel privileged to pass on to people who have the patience to learn. Quilting is not a lost art. New quilters do what we older quilters teach them. You know, we have a lot of choices in this life. We can choose to be happy or we can choose to be miserable and make everyone around us miserable. My purpose in life is to do the best I can and to help as much as I can in the time I have left to live. God has given us all gifts, and it behooves us to use them how we can.

"I like the old-fashioned-type quilts. But even in traditional quilting you have to have a little eye for color combination."

H a r r i e t   G i l e s

Harriet Giles weaves one-of-a-kind rag rugs, pillows, jackets, vests, and tote bags from her home on a horse farm in Lexington, Kentucky. She lives in a cottage with her husband, Ben, one of the farm's managers, and their two children, Mary and Woody, both of whom have already learned to weave small runners on the tiny antique looms Harriet has given them.

She's done it all for them. As a young mother who moved "back to the land" with her husband after college, Harriet origi-

nally sought a craft that would provide her a way to make a living and still permit her to stay at home to raise her children.

With no formal artistic training, but with a mathematical mind and the weighty influence of a mother who sewed and a grandmother who still hooks oriental-style rugs at age 97, Harriet found her perfect niche as a rug weaver.

Her "rag rugs" are anything but. She designs and weaves rugs in many sizes for her own customers and for clients of many of the finest interior design firms in Kentucky. She wove jackets for the "Oh! Kentucky" boutique at Bloomingdale's 1982 crafts promotion. But, of course, I am most proud of the rug Harriet designed and wove for me when I was First Lady of Kentucky. It is in the Kentucky Governor's Mansion in Frankfort.

The day I visited Harriet, she and I sat down at her huge two-person loom for an elementary course in weaving a room-sized rag rug. I had no idea how hard it was to work the loom. You have to throw the shuttle

back and forth and push pedals with your feet. I felt as if I were playing the organ.

I was humbled, however, when I watched Harriet's nine-year-old daughter Mary weave a beaded place mat on her own loom. Harriet's weaving is a true "cottage craft" already being passed down to the next generation.

I have no art background whatsoever. I grew up in Clark County, Kentucky, and at that time I think there was one art teacher for all the elementary kids in the whole county. I never took an art class. But I always enjoyed making things.

After college, my husband and I moved to Virginia. We lived way back up on top of a little mountain. You could say we were part of the back-to-the-land movement. We had a huge garden and grew our own food. We had three dozen chickens and occasionally raised a pig that we slaughtered ourselves. Because it was a real rural county, there were not that many jobs that

you could just leap into. There were a fair number of people who were supporting themselves at least partially by crafts. It just seemed like a natural thing for me to do. I went to a weaving workshop at a nearby college and finally decided I'd buy a floor loom. I didn't really start weaving on a serious basis until we moved to Kentucky. I had my first child here and was looking for a home project to satisfy my desire for something to do while I was at home raising children.

When I first started weaving I didn't intend to make rag rugs. I thought they were so simple and so plain. But rags are free. I thought, oh, I can just play around with these, and then I realized that there really are infinite possibilities to weave structures and color combinations and stripe sequences and the whole gamut of design. Even if you never weave anything but rag rugs you can never reach the design limits.

I set aside two mornings a week and started weaving on a serious basis. I explored a lot of different things before I wove my first rag rug. Then one day my husband came home from work and told me that one of his clients had asked him if he knew where she might find a room-size rag rug. I said, "How about me? I think I'm willing to try that."

It was an 8 1/2' x 15' rug and I wove it in three panels because my first loom was only 3 1/2' wide. I sewed them together, which was the traditional way of making them. It was a lot of fun making the rug. It had stripes that had to line up perfectly across the three panels. I had to teach myself how to measure very accurately. I had to determine how much it was going to shrink and a whole bunch of other things I had never done before. My husband actually lost his favorite yellow shirt in the last stripe, because I ran out of material.

This is not true of every rag rug woven, but a lot of the ones I've seen in shops are what I call "hit and miss," strips of rag woven together in a random fashion. My

rugs are different. I pay a lot more money than most rag rug weavers to get the right color strips. Mine are a lot more highly designed than other rag rugs and that's the fun of it, although I do like weaving, too. There's something about putting your body into a rhythmic motion that releases your mind to a very peaceful place of concentration. It can be like a meditation if your weaving is not something you have to concentrate on a great deal. Different pieces require different degrees of concentration. I have gone through different periods in the course of my weaving. I probably devoted two years to serious design work because when I first started I thought I would weave one-of-a-kind rugs. I thought that my customers would want to be a part of the process — that they would tell me

what kind of work they wanted and I would design something in line with that. But what happened was that most people couldn't visualize; they needed to see designs to compare and react against. That was true for production work and things I sold through stores and galleries as well as for custom work. They really preferred having a variety of options. So I came up with ten or twelve designs, including variations on those designs.

One interesting new market for me is the restoration and reproduction of rag rugs for old or historic houses. Unfortunately, original inventories are not often available and it bothers me to guess what floor covering might have been used. Or worse, to put a piece in a museum setting that merely captures an antique feeling, regardless of

"I'm a designer/weaver, production engineer, business manager, marketer/ advertiser, graphic artist, sometimes a mechanic, and a sales representative."

time period. I have been amazed to discover that a typical colonial rag rug was originally woven in vivid, bold colors rather than the muted, faded colors we associate with them. I hope to contribute to our understanding of the use and making of historic textiles.

I think that crafts and handmade things will survive because the more technological our society becomes, the greater need we have for handmade, simple things surrounding us in our homes. It gives us a cozy, simple homey feeling that we don't get anywhere else.

and coats for material. But I wanted a wider rug, so I decided I'd take some two-by-fours and build some kind of upright loom. It just seemed like it was in me to do it. I got the loom built and I started making my own clothing designs.

I get all my knowledge of how to do things by reading and talking to people and by putting things together in my head. I sit down with a pencil and paper and I work backwards. I think of a rug I want to weave that is fifteen feet by twenty feet, then I think out what I have to build to make what's in my head.

"If I know I'm going to need a fifteen-foot-wide reed and beater, I know that the rest of the loom is going to have to be at least sixteen feet. I had to make a loom that large, and still fit it in my house!"

I will share what I know with others. I figure if anybody asks me something three times they really want to know, so I'll tell them things. If they drive all the way out here to Log Cabin Lane through the Stargate to see me, they must really want to know. And I love to tell people how to do things.

A lot of people think that food only

comes from supermarkets, that water only comes from pipes. My own four children all can weave, spin, make soap, cook, they know about herb medicine, all of it. They really like the word I use — *feral*. It means having a certain wildness about you, the ability in your genetic makeup to make it, to like it, if someone dropped you into the wilderness alone.

Feral people prefer to make their own choices and they are happy with the choices they make. I think of myself as feral. I could live about anywhere in the universe. Whatever planet or cloud they'd drop me on, I would want to live there, and I would figure out a way to live there.

Following your own creative call is the easiest path in life. Just roll on your back and go with the flow — it's much easier. You don't have to do a thing but make yourself available to that greatest artwork of the universe — then it all just comes.

Whenever I weave a rug, I try to cause the viewers to experience the work through all of their senses. Using all five senses at once activates a person's sixth sense, and that's what I work for. The simplicity of it all is so beautiful. Wordsworth experienced all five senses when he looked at a single blade of grass.

When I'm making a rug for someone, I keep working the colors until the rug says "Yay-yuh!" If I can't get it to say "Yay-yuh!" then I cut it off the loom. If that rug goes out into the world unhappy, who knows what destruction will be wrought. There must be "agreement" in that rug, and from that comes joy all over the world.

"You don't have to pay $2500 for a walnut loom. You can just take some two-by-fours and build your own loom. The fabric is what matters, and I'll get the thread from somewhere. That's the real pioneer spirit."

A l m a   L e s c h

Alma Lesch's fabric collages have been winning regional and national art awards since the early 1950s, when she was a graduate student and teacher at the Art Center School in Louisville. As one of Kentucky's elder stateswomen of art, she is well respected not only by generations of her Kentucky art students, but also by art critics, collectors, and gallery owners across the country.

She is best known for her fabric "portraits" — collages of clothing and objects that create personality portraits of people. Some of her pieces in this style, "Uncle Bob," for example, are assembled from actual pieces of clothing and jewelry, personal items be-

longing to the person whose portrait she is creating. Others are assembled from objects Alma has collected over years of combing antique shops and vintage-clothing stores. Alma's popularity in arts-and-crafts circles around Kentucky is proof of people's fascination with her innate ability to join and assemble objects to create specific images.

Alma and her husband, Ted, live a quiet life in Shepherdsville, Kentucky. They have lived there since 1948 and like their small-town life. But Louisville is only thirty minutes away — convenient for trips to view some of her large fabric pieces hanging in the Meidinger Office Tower lobby, the Speed Building, the boardroom of Citizens Fidelity Bank, Saint Francis in the Fields Church, and the Macauley Theater, and to meet with art patrons and collectors who commission her work.

I do whatever I want to do. I always have. I grew up making things with my hands, from the very beginning. We lived on a farm. Because we were too far out, we made a lot of things we needed. But we didn't just slap them together. They had to be good-looking. I don't know whether that goes with having a good eye. I suppose I was born with one. And that was also in both families, the grandparents, and parents. I can remember somebody in the family would criticize somebody else if whatever they had done didn't come up to aesthetic expectations. They didn't use words like "aesthetic," but they would just say you made a mess.

I've always worked with fabrics, making clothes from grade school on up. I work all over the house. I grew up working wher-

96

ever I happened to be. I don't have to go to one place for my mind to think about art or for my hands to do it. I do have a comfortable place at home where I lay out some of the textile pieces that I'm working with because I need a table to put them on.

The actual fabricating of a piece is nothing but labor. I can handle it, but it's drudgery. The fun is in designing the piece and changing it and playing with it until you think you've gotten the most out of the materials that you're working with. That's my idea of fun.

I enjoyed teaching. I think that was my long suit — making the students aware. I taught them not to be afraid of anything they could think of, to use it. To start with something, whatever they could think of — to go with it in their design and to try it. I know it was one of the things that the students liked. It's having the confidence to do the crazy ideas that come to mind.

One of my main themes in textile work is making portraits from old clothing, vintage clothing. That idea came after I had been to an auction and purchased a lot of vintage, turn-of-the-century clothing. I was sorting it and playing with it and I just decided, why not make a portrait of the person that I had purchased the clothing from? And that's how it all started.

I know all the fabric techniques but what you can do with them is never complete. You can combine them if you need to. If you have knowledge and a background in surface design, you can combine the technical part of it with the eye — the artistic eye — and information that goes along with it. I don't think you ever reach a limit.

"You can do so much more with fabric than you can by putting paint on canvas. Maybe that's why painters put paper, leather, collage, and that sort of thing on canvas."

QUILTIN

here — the quilting and the basket making and the woodworking.

Here at David, we sell quilts, baskets, wooden items of all sorts. Right now we only have one local potter, so we are buying some things from someone in Morehead. We buy our spoons from Virginia Petty because we only have one person locally who does spoons and we can't keep enough of them here. Roy May is a wonderful woodworker who makes things for us. He is not too far from here. We have some artists. Tom Whittaker, from Magoffin County, teaches at Prestonsburg Community College and does watercolors for us. We have lots of quilters. Polly Justice is one of our best quilters. She doesn't live too far from here, just seven or eight miles. She does not quilt with a frame, she quilts with a hoop, and she loves talking to people. Her husband, Buck, used to make beautiful hickory-bark chairs.

Our basket makers, Colleen and Orville Messers, are wonderful. They are a great family. Their skill has been passed down for generations. Colleen also has a little weaving room in her home and many of the rugs and place mats we have here are hers. Their children are all in college or away or married right now, but they have all been involved in making things. Colleen and Orville bark chairs and stools, too. Jim Conley whittles in coal and does walking sticks. He carves faces from these little chunks of coal.

Our philosophy is that we are not necessarily here to make money, but for some people that is an important part of what we do. We just try to help people supplement their income and be proud of their work. The crafts center was first started to give people an outlet to sell their crafts — a reason to come out of their homes to meet people. Over the years a lot of that has been maintained. We have potluck sup-

pers about every other month and we always try to have a party at Thanksgiving and Christmas. We get together for special occasions. We try to celebrate together and share in each others' lives.

We are not just a place of business where people bring their things. We try to create as social and as pleasant an atmosphere as possible for people. Quilting and sewing are the skills we teach to people. We feel we are able to help younger people learn skills, and to help longtime quilters improve their skills, so that they can really sell what they are making.

Two-thirds of our people — at times as high as three-fourths of our people —are

ABOVE: The David quilt presented by the governor's office staff to the Browns for Christmas, 1982.

women. There is some wonderful talent here that often needs to be discovered and encouraged and helped along a little bit. I feel that what we are about is bringing out the talent and the beauty that is here.

A r t u r o   A l o n z o   S a n d o v a l

Arturo Alonzo Sandoval isn't a typical Kentucky artist or craftsman. He is a fiber genius, an innovator, a prolific, imaginative, and visionary artist whose "high-tech textiles" are very well known and respected throughout the United States. What distinguishes him from other artists working in fiber is that he weaves unusual twentieth-century materials into his pieces. Arturo creates his collages with everything from mylars and lurex to scraps, old microfilm and magnetic tape, which he weaves with fiber into fantastic metallic wall-hangings.

*Arturo teaches design at the University of Kentucky while pursuing his own personal expressions. "When I first came to the University, fifteen tornados had just hit Lexing-*ton. *Flying over the city I saw what I thought was a fabulous celestial vision, not realizing the airport was on fire. The next day, I explored my new home. I loved the campus immediately."*

Arturo's work has been collected and exhibited by hundreds of collectors, museums, and corporations. He has a piece in the permanent design collection of the Museum of Modern Art in New York.

Amid the fascinating and colorful debris of works-in-progress in his spacious studio, this fascinating man told me about his life.

I've been an artist ever since I was a child. I didn't really know what the future held for me, but I just wanted to create. The focus that I chose was textiles. I just felt very responsive to it. I really was excited by the processes. I was doing silk screening, block printing, batik, tie-dye. I was excited by the variety of expression and abstraction that you could get in a pattern. Textile design brought immediate results and it was very expressive. I could do so much with it. I took up weaving for the first time in grad school.

One evening while I was in the studio, about midnight, I had a spiritual experience. A voice told me that weaving would be very important to me. I remembered blacking out and then waking up. I looked around and there was no one there but me.

Then when I turned forty years old, I went to New Mexico, where I was born, and I discovered that all the men on my grandmother's side were weavers. I ran into the Cordova Weaving Shop — Cordova is my grandmother's maiden name — and all of a sudden here I was surrounded by weavers and all the men were my great-uncles and my cousins. I freaked out. I couldn't believe it. I really think that that voice in 1965 may have been some of the lineage telling me, "Arturo, weaving is important to you." I think that a lot of growth in this world is through faith, and

faith is believing. I believe that voice. I've worked hard to do what I think I should concerning that belief.

I'm fascinated by twentieth-century materials which combine to create what I call "high-tech textiles." I enjoy the beauty of these unbelievable materials that I call the miracle fabrics of our time.

My pieces should communicate messages directly and succinctly to audiences. That doesn't mean that a person with more sophistication won't see different levels of that message. I'll bring a totally naive person into my studio and I'll ask them to look at my work and tell me what they see. Usually they see what I intend. To me, art, even if it's abstract, should give you some sense of feeling. I've always wanted my pieces to do that, even in their most non-objective form.

Students need to know traditional color weaving. They need to see the beauty and the workmanship and the craft. That's what I had to learn — what to accept and what to reject. And that's really what it's all about, I think. I could do traditional weaving and be successful with it. But that's not what I'm into now. I'm talking about our culture. Being in America really is a blessing, because there's so much that we can do here — so much freedom.

Being in Kentucky allows me to have peace without all the distractions of the glitzy life. It allows me lots of work time. I love to teach, too. After six years of being here, I decided, You've got to teach, Arturo. So I've committed myself to teaching. If I were in New York, I'm sure I would be doing exotic things. But I'm sort of tickled that I'm here to share my creations with an audience that might never see it otherwise.

"Everything I do really is rooted in some kind of already-known technique. It's just a matter of re-experiencing it my way."

State of the Union No. 8, OLYMPIC GLORY

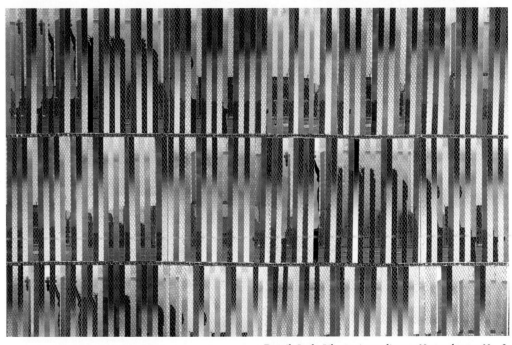

Detail, Lady Liberty According to Nostradamus No. 3

State of the Union No. 9, LANDSLIDE TO THE RIGHT

Ground Zero No. 4

meditative, a real soothing thing to do. Here I was with this little baby, you know, a mother for the first time, and sort of anxious and nervous about all of that. I managed to calm myself down through quilt making and I guess I got addicted.

The thing I didn't like at first about quilt making was piecing. I thought it was really boring. But I liked the notion of joining three layers together. So I started doing appliqué quilting. That led me into the art aspect of making quilts and I discovered I could use quilts not just as bed covers but as ways to express things.

It's a great joy for me to see quilts going from beds to walls. I know that quilts are art. Even the ones that were intended for the beds are art. We talk about how the modern art movement can be traced back to the old traditional quilts and their geometric designs. I'm not a geometric quilter, I'm a figurative appliqué artist. But I still treasure the tradition of quilt making.

Quilts bring people together. I accept commissions and I enjoy them because I find that I meet people and I learn about them. I try to make it very personal for them because I would want a piece to be very personal to me. All my work is personal. That's fun in a sense — surprising people with what your understanding of them is.

I've begun to notice that I am telling the story of my life with my quilts. I guess that's a neat thing to be able to say, that you spent your life telling the story of your life. I want people to look at my quilts and be able to see me. And even after I'm gone, my quilts will all still be here.

"I started looking at my life; maybe it was watching my own children grow. I spent a lot of time thinking about my own childhood. That's where my ideas come from."

Glass and Ceramics

David Keator

One of the most pleasant discoveries of my crafts journey awaited me last year when I visited an old textile-mill warehouse in the industrial Germantown area of Louisville and discovered the studio of ceramicist and furniture maker David Keator.

David has the rugged good looks of an athlete. In fact he was an athlete in high school, but went on to study ceramics in college and in some of the most prestigious graduate programs in the country.

David makes everything from tables, chairs, and porch swings to clocks, sconces, vases, containers, and fine ceramic dinnerware. His media? Fine woods, marble, and clay at the moment. His style? "Neoclassic eclecticism," he says, laughing. "elements of everything that interests me — Oriental, Art Nouveau, Deco. It's a hodge-podge, really."

Hardly a hodge-podge. Each piece reflects David's fine formal training and his meticulousness and attention to the intricacies of color, grain, texture, and design. Everything he makes is unique, never repeated by this serious artist.

Despite his seriousness, David describes himself as a "hopeless romantic." He recently made a purple-heart and pine porch swing, for his girlfriend , Tracey Clyatt.

At thirty-seven, with years of studying and teaching behind him, David now devotes all his time to his craft. He has developed a recognizable style and his pieces are now in the collections of Elton John, Richard Simmons, Kenny and Maryanne Rogers, and, of course,

Phyllis George! David's talents and his future are limitless.

I don't think I was born an artist. I went to art school. I was initially involved with printmaking mainly because I had a lot of two-dimensional design work in high school, so I thought that's what I wanted to do. In my second year of college a friend of mine took me over to this ceramics studio. I looked around and thought, You can draw with this, you can paint with this, you can throw a piece away if you make a mistake. It doesn't cost a lot of money. You can also make three-dimensional objects. The clay seemed like a very personal material and I liked working with my hands. I changed my major and started taking ceramics.

I went on to graduate school at the New York State College of Ceramics at Alfred University, and later to the Penland School of Crafts in North Carolina as a resident artist. As I look back on it, I can't explain why I ended

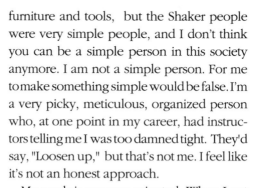

up in art. It just felt right. I was happy doing it.

I ended up moving to Louisville to teach at the Louisville School of Art until they closed it. When I stopped teaching ceramics, I was bound and determined I was going to start doing a lot of architectural interiors. I tried to get people to let me do samples — fireplaces, entranceways, tile floors, anything. And I started doing furniture as a way of structuring those architectural concerns. Now I'm doing furniture because it's different, very contemporary and really bold. And it's something nobody else is doing because I involve the ceramic pieces. Initially the furniture making started as a way to display the clay work I was doing — I made elaborate pedestals. They evolved into tables, and the tables led to chairs — now I'm mostly doing furniture.

I like the tactile qualities of a lot of different materials, and I like the fact that a beautiful object can also be functional. I like a thing that you can use whether it looks like it should be used or not; the fact that it can be touched, that there's a lid on it — that's an experience, taking a lid off. I used to design a lot of my lids so you weren't sure whether they came off. It was always a surprise. Using art and craft you can make an incredibly beautiful piece that demands to be touched.

Because of my art school background, I can say that my work is derived from art. But there is also a lot of craft in my work. I can't have one without the other. I really like Shaker furniture and tools, but the Shaker people were very simple people, and I don't think you can be a simple person in this society anymore. I am not a simple person. For me to make something simple would be false. I'm a very picky, meticulous, organized person who, at one point in my career, had instructors telling me I was too damned tight. They'd say, "Loosen up," but that's not me. I feel like it's not an honest approach.

My work is process-oriented. When I get an idea, I sit down and fill up a page with little thumbnail sketches. I work the idea until it starts to evolve, to work itself into certain elements. But then things will change because I allow them to change. I will interchange every possible element I can think of until that piece really starts to sing, and then it goes together. Of course, the finished product is always the icing on the cake. If it's a piece of furniture, it goes home and it lives with me for two weeks and it gets moved around and I look at it every day and I ask myself, "What do I really like about it? Is there something that I could have done better?"

I stay fresh because I force myself to change. My life is on a three-year cycle. It always has been. Every three years I just start to grow into something different. It is almost a predestined change.

Obviously I have a need to express myself. I can look at what I did six years ago and tell you exactly where my life was just by looking at that piece. I'm much more at ease since I've become my own boss. I'm doing what I want to do, and the work is starting to reflect a kind of airy, whimsical, even nonsensical approach to life.

"I came up with a new phrase to describe my work: Neo-Classic Eclecticism. It's Art Deco, Oriental, and a little Art Nouveau. You can't help being eclectic in this day and age."

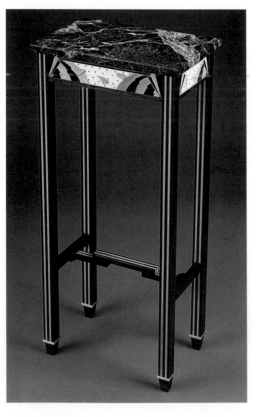

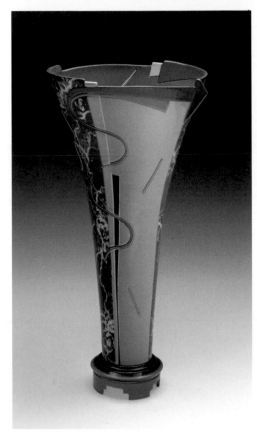

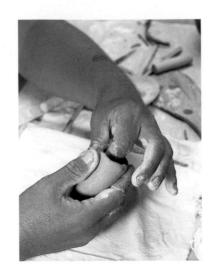

W a y n e   F e r g u s o n

Wayne Ferguson typifies the young Kentucky ceramicist of today: talented, dedicated to his craft, knowlegeable and respectful of ceramics' history and tradition, but branching out in new, imaginative, non-traditional directions.

Take one look at his clay creations and it's clear he is not interested in mimicking the old forms. It's also clear that this is a guy with a wacky sense of humor who enjoys evoking a laugh from his viewers.

Wayne does things his own way and, he will frankly tell you, he's not in it for the money. In fact, he has devoted much of his time over the last fifteen years to teaching pottery workshops to handicapped people

and kids in the Kentucky public schools.

Wayne's own children — eight-year-old Laurel and ten-year-old Lindon Redbird — are also important to him. I was really touched by his description of what must be every artist-parent's dilemma: "My concern about my kids right now is that they understand why I'm an artist and why I'm not making a lot of money. Are they going to respect me for the contribution I make culturally and forgive me for the lack of money? That's the problem of having two kids when you're doing what I'm doing. I hope they'll appreciate it in time."

I 've whittled some, but that's not for me. It's a subtractive process, and I can't deal with it. I've got to be adding and building. As you get a little bit older and you've been doing this for a little while, you've got to stick with what you're best at, and for me that's working with clay.

Being a professional potter is not an easy

thing to do, because I don't want to make functional production products. I like to make things that are very personal, maybe even psychologically expressive, and a lot of times they're not going to sell. But that's where my work has taken me.

A lot of times my things don't even resemble pots. Basically, I like to manipulate the clay and put it together in such a way that somebody who doesn't know the first thing about ceramics can look at it and react to it. Usually it's a reaction that's a positive response. I mean, they think it's funny, and that's fine with me — I think it's funny, too. But I don't really want to try to make something that's so mysterious that only another ceramic artist can understand it. I like to make things that are a little bit humorous, childlike maybe.

I think my ceramic animals with whistles in them were mostly influenced by [Kentucky wood carver] Edgar Tolson. I lived about twenty-five miles from him, and every time his agent came through town, he would pick me up and we'd go down to visit with Edgar. In a sense, there is a connection between folk-art carvings and my animal forms. I'm not trying to make something that's realistic. But I could never be a folk artist. I've gone to college. The fact is that I've been, I hate to say, contaminated; I've seen and done too much. In my opinion folk artists are people who haven't seen too much and who have a vision that's localized, centralized, coming from themselves. The things that they create are often coming out of the fact that they are isolated.

It's very important to me that my things change. I had a kid come up here the other day. He must have been ten years old. He said, "You shouldn't put gorillas on everything." And it made me think, well, he's right. I'm going to change that.

I struggled with the humor of my work for a while. There's a thin line between being cute and being humorous. Every now and then I deliberately make a piece that's less humorous. But other times I enjoy getting a grin out of people who come by. I laugh a lot when I'm making these things, so I figure somebody else should enjoy them, too.

I like working with clay. I've never used a sketchbook. I like sitting down with the material itself and putting hours of time in on a piece, then sitting back and looking at it, realizing that this came from my skills, my hands, my background. If I've done it right, it's not going to look like anybody else's work. It's going to be my signature.

"The unsophisticated look of my animal forms is deliberate. I want them to have a little bit of a connection with cartoons. I like the animals to be childlike and a little bit animated, but I'm not really trying to make something that looks exactly like that particular animal."

R o n   K i n g

Sometimes terrible tragedies in our lives can trigger creative rebirths. The turning point in Ron King's life was a tornado that ravaged Kentucky and southern Ohio in 1974, destroying Ron's family home and blowing much of his life away. His home gone, Ron found himself emotionally detached from much of what had held his life together — his job, his brand-new car, and ultimately, his marriage. Ron looked upon the tornado as a "message" to follow his dream of pursuing a career as a glass artist. At the time, he had been taking graduate art classes at the University of Cincinnati and had grown increasingly interested in art glass. He thought, while all the cards were in the air anyway, he would reshuffle them into a new artistic life, so he took the insurance money he collected on his share of the house and moved to Louisville, Kentucky.

Ron now lives a few blocks from his glass studio in the Butchertown area of downtown Louisville. He intentionally owns no car and few "things" and has none of his art glass in his home, because he thinks he would be too critical of his pieces if he kept them around.

His glass can be found in doors and windows in homes and businesses all over the area. A commissioned three-dimensional piece is in the permanent collection at the corporate headquarters of Kentucky Fried Chicken. Ron has had numerous panels and sculptures in regional museums, shows, and gallery exhibits.

He claims his best glass piece hasn't been made yet. "If you had made your best piece," he says, smiling, "then you would quit." Ron King is not about to quit because he still loves the way sunlight "breaks into a thousand rays" when it hits a piece of his glass.

We asked him, however, what would be in the final chapter of the book of his life. He responded immediately: "He took a vacation in Maine."

I really like the fact that glass projects. It's two-dimensional and three-dimensional at the same time. The light passes through, projecting away from its surface. It's the only thing that I have found that does that. You're working, not with a thing, but with shadow, a reflection.

I think one must enjoy both the creative and production end of this work. If I had to choose between them, it would be very difficult. At this point I don't think I would be very happy doing one or the other. I'd rather design and execute my own work. There's a lot to be learned in doing the execution. Even in a very simple panel that you're working on, you can give yourself a problem to be solved, either a craft or a design problem. Something, you know, to keep up your interest in it, to further your

knowledge of it. But I like the hands-on thing, bugging around in the studio. I like to bevel it, sandblast it, acid it.

Louisville was a center of the glass community in the late 1800s. They did a lot of really good architectural glass here — church glass, Victorian glass, nice, very well-executed work, with great crafts people. Unfortunately, much of Louisville's art glass has been stripped out of some of the fine houses in Old Louisville.

I salvage glass a lot. I am one of these guys that goes to demolition sites, dumpsters — wherever I can get it. I spend a certain amount of my time experimenting with materials, looking for new materials. Sometimes the new materials are actually old materials. Another artist and I strip buildings that are being torn down or altered in some way. Finding materials is always a difficult thing for a glass artist.

How long does it take to make a piece? It all depends on what you're talking about. To complete a panel like this, I can start in the morning, design it, lay it out, cut the patterns, cut the glass, glaze it, cement it, and do it in an eight-to-ten-hour day. When you get into experimental design, because you have to stop a lot to reflect on what's going on, that takes some time. I use a glass

121

table so I can actually lay the panel down on the table, walk down the steps beneath it, and take a look up through the glass to see what's going on in relation to patterns and colors.

To me, working with glass is a very personal thing. Financially it's not rewarding and there's really no status involved in it. You pretty much deal with yourself in this small circle of people who are doing similar things, and that's where your encouragement and gratification comes from. If you're a curious individual and you just want to explore something that is basically unknown, then it's a fascinating enterprise. Glass has been with us several thousand years now, and still it has not been explored completely. There are plenty of things left to be discovered, and I would encourage people to head in that direction.

"I am fascinated by the changes that light goes through when it passes through glass and I am actually more interested in random than programmed light. Glass is very sensitive to natural-light movement. It really demands that natural light. As natural light moves, it changes. You never see the same thing twice."

S a r a h   F r e d e r i c k

If you ask Sarah Frederick to describe herself, she will respond that she is a Kentucky potter, a craftsperson, a mother, a householder, a gardener, an environmentalist. She is a lover of landscapes who always wanted to write stories but found fiction too arduous. Sarah believes that clay is her proper medium, and she uses her skills as a potter to tell "more pictorial" stories about things she sees in her environment.

Sarah's love for plants and organic forms has surfaced in many of her latest pieces — teapots that look like melons with tiny fruits as lids; containers shaped like gourds; oil lamps that resemble apples. They are all colored by Sarah's technique of atomizing glazes and glaze stains onto dark clays.

Though formally trained in college, her career as a potter didn't blossom until she divorced "at the end of my third decade." She has become one of Kentucky's most famous and most prolific potters. Her pieces have been shown and purchased by individuals and galleries all over the country.

Sarah's pottery studio in Louisville is a sky-lit converted garage nestled in the middle of her well-tended backyard garden. She is the mother of two — a son, Louis, who is studying acting in college, and a daughter, Mia, who is following in her mother's footsteps by attending art school in California.

The trail began, for me, in California. I was going to Mills College, majoring in painting, drawing, and sculpture. I always thought I would be an artist when I grew up. I found myself at one point in a class called Basic Crafts. My teacher was a man named Tony Prieto, who, luckily enough, was in the forefront of the contem-porary crafts movement in the United States. The studio had wonderful, huge gas-fired kilns. There was a potters' guild and wonderful work was being done. The guy was just fabulous.

I just fell for clay right away. Clay is a natural medium in this part of the country because a lot of clay is mined here. A lot of rural potters can go out their back door and dig clay. I haven't found that practical, because most of my working life has been in Louisville. But it's an important folk craft for this area. There are quite a few potters in Kentucky.

To me, pottery's got two things going for it — form and surface color. The kind of clay work I started in was really abstract, in that it was just a form with glaze on it. My initial thrill was feeling the clay, making the pottery. Then there was a spell when the end of the process was more interesting, the glazing. When I was doing a lot of dipping and pouring of glazes, the physical nature of the glazing was most exciting. The surface was what was important. Now

I've gotten into a very tight way of decorating my pieces. I'm using this noisy airbrush and compressor and I'm again in a phase where the making part is the most fun. It goes in a cycle. You've got the making, the firing, and the final decorating and glazing. It's a little bit scary because you've done all this work and the final part is what will make or break the whole piece.

I think a lot of people take basic techniques of pottery and then run with them as an art form. But you don't learn to make pots without doing it for years — doing a lot of different forms and doing them over and over. I was invited to be in a teapot show recently. I thought I was doing some fabulous teapots, but when I look at slides and pictures of the early ones I did, I can't believe it. I really think that working in the way I'm working, doing things over and over and over, is really the only way to get good at it. I think that's true with anything. One artist I knew talked about how, when you get an idea, you have to kind of work it through to completion, and when you've done that, you're kind of through with it. I'm still working on some things that I'm not through with. I probably will never be through with the landscape. The landscape is, and I guess always has been, my basic turn-on. It seems so natural to me, but I think that it's different for everybody. I start with what I see and it's like it goes in my eyes and comes out my hands. And when it's going really well, and when the work's coming out fast, it's terribly exciting.

I'm making jars and bowls and traditional teapots, pottery forms, functional vessels that do function, that can work. But they will often have a glaze on them that isn't really appropriate for everything. I don't make what I would call utilitarian things, but I do make vessels and that is, I find, what I want to do. When I was doing a lot of landscape work and a lot of painting —

two-dimensional images on things — I wasn't as happy. For a couple of years I made plates and bowls strictly to paint images on. I got really good at making plates and I got real good at making bowls. I'm happier now that I make more objects that work. Not that plates and bowls don't work, but the main reason for making the plates and bowls was to paint images on them. I've taken some of the images that I once painted and made pots into those things, like flowers and organic forms. Currently, since I don't have a landscape to look at, I look at smaller things. I look at things out of my garden a lot.

I'm glad pottery is the way I earn my living. I'm *definitely* glad it's the way I earn my living. What I'm trying to conquer now, though — now that I know how to make it work as a living — is how to control the beast. I have to keep it from running my life, so that I can enjoy it, and coordinate it with other things in my life, like tending to my plants, having a garden, doing the things I like to do around the house.

I ran into a person at a street fair in New York who had bought one of my small oil lamps in Kentucky and told me she loved it and used it. I like that feeling. I like the feeling that my things are in people's homes, and that, even if they are using them as one would use a mug or a soup bowl, they are enjoying my piece. They often let me know.

"I think my colors and surface ideas are unique — a combination of usefulness and playfulness and style."

Greg Seigel

You previously met quilt maker Rebekka Seigel in the Textiles chapter. Her husband, Greg, is a potter who hand-fires distinctive pieces from clay he finds near their farm outside Owenton, Kentucky.

Greg's pottery is whimsical and humorous and obviously inspired by his life on the farm. Alligators, fish, frogs — his pottery is alive with animal influences.

Each piece of Greg's pottery is fired to about twenty-five hundred degrees Fahrenheit, at which time Greg throws salt into the kiln's firebox. The salt then gives off sodium vapor, which adheres to the pottery and reacts with the clay and glazes to give each piece a distinctive look and feel. Greg is particularly proud right now of the new brick kiln he just built in the side yard of his home — something he could never have done when he lived in Cincinnati.

Greg will tell you that living in the country, making a living from crafts, has its sacrifices and is not an easy life. But he and Rebekka have chosen that life and they wouldn't trade it for the world.

Some of the first artistic influences I remember were in my grandfather's basement. He was a metal worker who made machines and invented all kinds of things. He had a little brick kiln in his basement that my brother and I used to play with. I liked the fire. I liked the color of the kiln. That was really my first experience with clay.

Every time I pick up a piece of clay, it's a new piece of clay. I don't measure anything. I know a lot of potters divide their clay into little lumps that weigh exactly so many pounds. I don't do any of that. If I start out to make a cup that's straight-sided and tall, and I lift the clay incorrectly from the bottom, it'll end up short and wide, and I don't care.

I like to think, when I work with clay, that I am making something that has never been made before. Even though cups were made before, this handle is my own style handle. Although this is a regular cup, it has a definite one-of-a-kind quality because of the way the salt hits one side versus the other. Even if I made five of these the same way, they'd all look different by the time they came out of the kiln. I really like the one-of-a-kindness of it. That's the art for me. Plus I have a sense of humor and I like people to think that my things are funny.

Some people say that potters are either mud men or fire men. The mud guys like to make them and don't like to do anything else with them, and the fire guys like to fire pots but don't really like making them. I am a mud guy sometimes and a fire guy sometimes. I like the whole process. When I'm doing one, I like that exclusively; and when I'm doing the other, I like that exclusively. Sometimes it's hard to change back and forth, but that's part of my adventure with this material.

Most people today use electric kilns. I call it toaster ware. It's just like a giant toaster. They put it in and have total control over what it's going to look like. They have zero losses. They make a helluva lot more money than I do. But their things are not "fired." I really like the marks on the bottom of my pieces where they were stilted in the kiln. My fingerprints show on most pieces where I held the piece upside down with my thumb while glazing it. I really like the traditional fire aspect of pottery a lot, and the marks that the fire makes.

There are two pieces in the kiln right now that I haven't seen. They are functional because they're cups, but they are art, too, because of the statements they make. I like to do both art and utility pieces. I recently read an article where the author was comparing "art" to "craft," and the author ended up using the term "craft art." I think that's probably the way I would describe myself, too, as a craft artist. I want people

to use my stuff, but I really like to think I've made something special out of what is ordinary clay.

I love where we live and how we live. There's no one I really want to trade places with. I don't want to be president, or somebody else making pots. I love what I do for a living, and I get to play music, I get to draw, and I get to walk in the woods. I have a pretty great life.

F r e d   d i   F r e n z i

Fred Maurer, also known as Fred di Frenzi, has been called the "mentor of the art-glass movement in Kentucky." "That's because I was the first one to do hot glass in the area," he says modestly. As Fred will tell you, he was first "seduced" into glass as an art medium while he was in graduate school at the University of Illinois. He brought the medium home to Kentucky in the late 1970s when, with the help of a grant from the National Endowment for the Arts, he became an artist-in-residence at the Louisville School of Art. He built a shed for a classroom, scrounging materials from old buildings, installed a glass-melting furnace, and began experimenting with glass blowing.

When the school moved two years later,

Fred began a three-and-a-half-year stint as a singer, songwriter, and bass guitarist for the rock group Jil Thorp and the Beat Boys. Fred Maurer became Fred di Frenzi the evening of the band's first paid performance. He removed the favorite shirt he was wearing and looked at the shirt's label, which said "Florenza." The name evoked the image of Italy, famous for its glass blowing. Considering himself a "frenzied performer," he decided to change his name and, at that moment, became Fred di Frenzi.

The new name became the trademark for a line of fused-glass jewelry he sold on the road, and he has continued to use it professionally as a glass sculptor and artist. Over the past five years, Fred has been experimenting with new glass designs and hot-glass techniques. His pieces have been exhibited in glass shows and galleries all over the country and are in the permanent collections of the Kentucky Fried Chicken and Coca-Cola corporate headquarters here in Kentucky and in the First National Bank of Louisville.

Fred, his wife, Nancy Carrington, and their newborn son live in the heart of Middletown, Kentucky, "within two miles" of every place Fred has lived and worked since he has been in Kentucky.

I went to graduate school so that I could keep making art in some sort of arena that was financially supportive. I got involved with glass and loved it. It's a seductive material if you like that heat, that spontaneity. There's no other material that can offer the range of possibilities that glass does. Glass is a really great sculptural material. The glass I'm doing now is different from the glass I did when I first got introduced to it, which was pouring molten glass out of a furnace and developing forms out of it — traditional forms. But the more you see of glass, the more you see different aspects. Glass holds a myriad of two-dimensional and three-dimensional possibilities. Its intrinsic beauty and preciousness can be exploited or denied, exagger-

ated or rejected, revered or spoofed.

Craftspeople are becoming more and more concerned with the kinds of ideas that sculptors and painters have. They're becoming influenced by the fine arts. My work could be in wood, it could be a painting, it could be in stone. It's a classic sculptural format. Now, where the craft comes in, I think, and where people start to perceive it as a craft, is that some of my glass things are taking on references to bowls, references to utilitarian kinds of vessels. But there's nothing specifically useful about my pieces. It's getting harder to discern what separates craft from art because a lot of these craftsmen, I think,

just got tired of hearing that their work didn't earn any recognition in the world of art. The craftspeople are starting to use their traditional formats and their ways of working and are getting in contact with what sculptors and painters have always dealt with in their work.

Glass making really does fit into the craft category real well because it has the right kind of background — it's made by hand. I like glass because it has so much emotional depth. We take it for granted — looking through windows, not even thinking about it. But look at a piece of broken glass. If you accidentally break a piece of glass in the bathtub, there are all kinds of

things that start to work in your mind. There is a subconscious idea of what glass is. I like it for that reason. It is very rich; I like the fragility of it, and the fact that it cuts. It can be a dangerous material. I like it also because people don't really understand how it's made.

What's going on with glass is what's going on with the whole movement in objects these days. We're seeing objects becoming heightened again. There's an awareness of handmade things. For the last twenty years we've gotten away from that. I think we're seeing a renewed interest and awareness that there can be content and there can be meaning in craft objects.

I like folk art. I've just been traveling around in the last year and a half or so, visiting some Kentucky folk artists and talking with those people, and that's a new direction, a new sphere of influence for me. My glass sculpture was pretty much abstract, but what I'm starting to do now is the kind of figurative and narrative pieces that carvers and folk artists have always done. And, in my new work, I'm showing the influence of Kentucky folk artists. Going around visiting them, talking with them, having them show you what they're doing — it's just great. They're just delightful people. I can definitely trace a big influence from Kentucky in my new work.

I think when you work in a creative field, you are capable of experimenting with a variety of expressive ideas and art forms. One of them is music. I got involved with the rock band because it was something that I'd always wanted to do. I really liked making music because it's the most successful way of collaborating in an art form. You can't get that in glass making. You can't get that in visual arts. Getting a cohesive sound from a group of people was an exhilarating experience.

There are days when I'd swap identities with someone else, someone wealthy and famous. On other days, when the ideas are clear, the design is strong and the mishaps are minimal, that's when I'm perfectly content with what I make and who I am.

"I'm working with the imagery of things. My new series is figurative, kind of portraiture in a way. But then I'm messing with the simplicity of it by sticking something in the background of these 'portraits.' That gets everybody's mind moving."

B y b e e   P o t t e r y

Bybee Pottery is a tradition in Kentucky. I fell in love with their distinctive pottery the first time I saw it, and the more I learn about it, the more I love it.

Bybee is the oldest existing pottery west of the Alleghenies. For over a century the pottery has been fired in a log barn in Bybee, Kentucky, in the southern hills of Madison County. The building itself is a historical treasure. The floor level has been raised several inches above the original by over a century's worth of dust from the clay.

The Cornelison family, now in its fifth generation of ownership, makes pottery just as grandfathers Webster, James Eli, Walter, and Earnest Cornelison did in the past: by mining the clay, mixing it with water, grinding it in the old pug mill, then throwing and shaping it on the potter's wheel. It has always been a family operation. The sixth generation is preparing to take over for the next hundred years.

On a beautiful spring day, I talked to Walter Cornelison as he made trademark Bybee coffee cups on his potter's wheel.

I asked my grandmother one day, "What was my great, great-grandfather's occupation?" She said he was a potter here. Years later, I realized that there were three or four pottery families in a radius of three or four miles. Legend has it that the people of Boonesboro found this clay many years ago. Out of pure necessity they started using it. It's very pure, clean clay. It has been filtered, cleaned, screened more or less, and it's laying there in a vein right on top of white sand. We dig our clay in the fall of the year, generally, hoping the water table is down just a little bit.

Our family is pretty much occupied here. My daughter will work here in the summer. She is a teacher, but her husband works here. I've got two sons who work here. They both have other occupations but they work here, basically. There's never been any pressure put on any one of them to stay or even start to work here. I would hate to see the business go to some other owners, but, by the same token, I realize that each generation has to do its own thing. You have to like this work. You have to have a feel for it. I like to think of it as a community project, because local people have worked in the pottery business a long time. We've had people work here whose families have worked here for three generations.

134

of ridiculous for us to talk about production here. But we have orders we have to fill and time schedules. We're approximately four years behind with our dinnerware orders. It doesn't make a bit of sense to business people. They say, why don't you increase production? Simply because Bybee Pottery is and has been known as handmade pottery. If you increase production, then you have to have more clay. You have to have more facilities for that clay. You have to have more people to do it. Then you have to have more kiln space, and the first thing you know, you're becoming commercial. We feel like the day that they can put a stamp of commercialism on us will be the day of our demise. We would not be able to compete with commercial potteries. Frankly, we don't want to. We like to think that someone handles every piece of pottery at least one time as it goes through.

It's almost second nature with us, going along and checking pieces of pottery, and maybe we'll see a little something, a little speck on it. We try to watch it from the first stage until it's finished. My wife and my oldest son, Buzz, are down there, and they see it last. My other son, Jim, is almost a swing employee. He is responsible for digging the clay but he can fit into any place along the production line. I kind of like that idea because the day's coming when somebody has to take over, and if that person has been stuck in one spot, and that's all he knows, he'll be lacking in the other steps, the middle steps in pottery making. So we like for everyone to get involved from the beginning to the end.

Our business has evolved slowly. Each person has contributed something, and I feel very fortunate to have the family background that I have. Each generation has left its mark even though we've made different types of pottery. I'll add my part to it and then hand it off to another generation.

Although we have been around a long time, we have certainly introduced new things over the years. As the needs change, we have been able to change with them. Each season, with fashions and things, colors change. If a certain shape that we are making doesn't seem to be in demand anymore, we just discontinue it for a while. The customers help us. We'll come up with a new idea, and they'll come in and say, Will you special order this for me? Will you make this to my dimensions? If we think we can produce it within the price range, we'll try it. We may make two or three at first and all of a sudden that piece will catch on and we'll put it in production. The word production is kind of a joke here. It's kind

S t e p h e n   P o w e l l

Many Americans became familiar with Kentucky glass artist Stephen Powell when he was featured on CBS's "Sunday Morning" television show. I had seen Stephen's work in galleries and in private homes in Kentucky, but I didn't meet him until the spring of 1988, when I visited his studio-classroom at Centre College in Danville, Kentucky. He showed me the technique of glass blowing, which, I must admit, is one of the crafts industry's most spectacular shows.

More impressive than the process to me, however, was the huge array of glass pieces sitting on the floor of Stephen's packing room. There were vivid colors, shapes, sizes

— seeing them all together showed me immediately Stephen's range and his terrific color sense, and why many experts consider him one of this country's finest new craftsmen.

Stephen admits he has put his artistry first in his life for a long time. I must brag on him a little bit here, though. Stephen is also one of the top tennis players in Kentucky in the senior division. How does he explain his rare combination of talents? "I like physical things, working with my hands. Glass and athletics are a perfect blend. It's all movement, how you move with the glass."

With the heat and noise from the glass kiln providing a dramatic background for our visit, Stephen told me all about working with glass.

When someone asks me what I do and I say I'm a glass blower, the first thing they think is that I make swans in the mall. But what I do is the real thing. For me the process of making the art or craft or whatever you want to call it is the most important thing. Other people

will tell you the idea is the most important. The process of ceramics, for example, always fascinated me. I liked the spontaneity, how you handled it, using your hands directly instead of chiseling the piece or whatever. And I liked the fire, the high temperatures, and what they can do to the material.

When I saw glass, I understood that it was just like ceramics. They are very closely related. My glass evolved out of my ceramics — in fact, I worked a lot of ideas I had in ceramics into glass, and vice versa. Centering on a potter's wheel gave me a tremendous advantage in glass. I spend a lot of time rolling a pipe on a bench, centering the glass. It's almost the same as centering on a wheel, even though glass is even more spontaneous than clay, it's a quicker medium.

I work transparency a lot on my pieces. I work stripes that might go in opposite directions on each side of a piece, so that when you look through you see the back side at the same time as the front. You get an interplay of lines and color matches. Transparency is probably what most glass artists push.

But there are lots of different approaches.

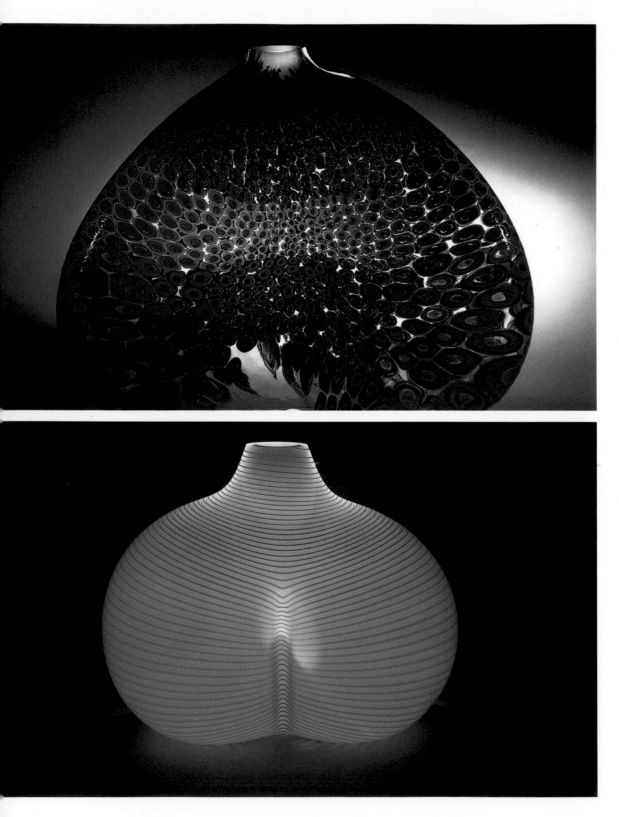

My style is simply vessel oriented. I make blown-glass vessels with figurative references. I put a lot of emphasis on color and the way light works on the color, either reflecting off or going through the piece.

Teaching pretty much takes up the whole day. I have nights to work and prepare. I really don't get that much of my own work done in a full semester. Summer is my major time to work — ten to twelve hours a day, doing nothing but glass. There's something really refreshing about students — those young minds. I talk to them about my work, get ideas from them, and some of them are my assistants.

When I'm in the studio, if everything is going right, I'm totally absorbed. It's probably the closest thing I've found to meditation or therapy. When I'm on, making that glass, it may last for only forty-five minutes, but it's a very satisfying time.

I feel my work is still evolving. I never have trouble with new ideas. I have a huge backlog of new ideas just ready to go. I've never had an artistic drought. I can't get to all the things I want to do. I am continually exploring what is basically a simple approach — making different forms and then relating surface designs to those forms.

Glass is, no pun intended, a "hot" medium right now. It's very strong. There are galleries that are exclusively about glass. I feel like I'm riding the crest of the wave at about the right time. Glass is a significant medium, and I think it's going to leave its mark in art history.

I've put glass first in my life for a long time. That's probably why I'm not married. I've probably pushed too hard in some directions and missed some things in life. But despite the recognition and attention I have gotten in the last few years, I've never felt that I was extremely talented. I've had to work real hard to accomplish everything that I have done.

Baskets

J e n n i f e r   H e l l e r

There are people you meet who strike you immediately as peaceful and happily focused in life. Jennifer Heller is one of those people. When I met her I was struck by her natural beauty — her shiny black hair, her flawless complexion, and her white teeth. Right away I felt that she cared deeply about the way she lives her life as a lover of nature and natural things.

She and her husband and son live a quiet life on a farm near Lexington, Kentucky. She has done everything from weaving

shawls from her own sheep's fleece to canning vegetables to building the house they live in. But she is now known in craft circles as one of Kentucky's best practitioners of willow-bark basket weaving.

On the way to Jennifer's home, we took a rather bumpy road. We saw a young boy walking down the road and stopped to ask, "Does Jennifer Heller live down here?" He said, "Sure! I'm her son." And he jumped in the car without even asking us who we were or what we wanted. That little boy was so innocent and uninhibited. He struck me in a very special way. Later his mother told us, "Ezra never meets a stranger."

Over some Lemon Zinger tea in her kitchen, Jennifer told me her story.

Once or twice a year I go down to Estill County where I used to live on the Kentucky River and strip bark for four or five days. The willows there just grow like weeds. I take only the ones that are the right size and have a good

straight trunk and aren't too close to the river. I take an ax, score around the tree; then I take a drawknife and get the bark started and then grab it with both hands and rip it off.

The first strips are short; then they get longer and longer until your last strip — which is the best strip — gets about forty or fifty feet long and it gets hung up. So you have to tug and tug, and usually it's a good idea to have someone tugging along with you, especially if you've been at it all day.

After I strip it, I load it all into the boat, go back to the boat dock, and then peel it. That's the most time-consuming part of it. Then I roll it up and lay it in the sun for about five days. I get it good and dry before I store it. I take a roll and soak it in the sink for about an hour and a half. Then I cut it into strips and weave it.

A group of us got into it at the same time. When I was about seventeen we were sitting on the riverbank resting, and we started peeling the tree bark up, and we thought, hey, this stuff is neat, real long and flexible. We started peeling the outer bark off and started brainstorming over what we could do with it. A girl friend of mine suggested we do some baskets. We had never done baskets before.

I love producing the baskets and I enjoy seeing them pile up. I put them over in the corner and in the evening I can look at them over there and decide what I want to do differently. I get most of my weaving done in the winter, because when spring hits I've got a big garden and lambing to do. I have to try to keep everything mowed, and I freeze and can. I still weave a little in the summer when I can get a day free.

I just did my two hundred and fifty-seventh basket. I average about thirty baskets a year now because I am only weaving part-time.

I use my baskets and I know a lot of the craftspeople I've traded with over the years use theirs. I think a lot of the people who buy my baskets display them. When they pay around a hundred dollars for a basket I don't think they want to get it dirty out in the garden.

My baskets are unique. There's almost nobody else doing this aside from the ladies in the little community where I used to live. The ladies there would all get together and have basket-weaving parties. We'd all go down to the swimming hole and soak our bark. Out of that group of ladies there are only two or three left who are weaving willow-bark baskets.

I have done other crafts, like spinning and weaving, but basket weaving has always seemed like the best manifestation of my love for nature. I've always been a nature girl, a flower child. I feel closely attuned to the earth and weaving seems like a natural offshoot of it. It was by chance that we discovered the willow bark. I just enjoy working with it so much. I am so enchanted by the final product. It is a real neat feeling that I haven't ever gotten over.

Curtis Alvey
The Basket Barn

The baskets I own are some of my most treasured things. I'm addicted to baskets, and those made by Curtis Alvey and his basket makers at the Basket Barn in Elizabethtown, Kentucky, have always been among my favorites.

I met Curtis in my early days in Kentucky. I probably have bought more baskets from Curtis than from anyone. I see Curtis at all the crafts fairs, and he comes to my after-Derby garden parties at Cave Hill Place to show his baskets and the art of making them to my out-of-town guests.

Curtis is as easy to like as a favorite easy chair. There's nothing false or pretentious about him. His upbringing in a basket-oriented crafts community set the tone for

his life and his future work in baskets.

Curtis learned to make baskets from his parents, who had been in the basket making business for over forty years. But Curtis is an entrepreneur with a business to run, so for many years he has utilized the hands of many Kentucky craftspeople to keep up with the thousands of orders he gets every year. As Curtis says, "We've got baskets in every state of the Union and a few foreign countries. They're in Neiman-Marcus, and I recall Bloomingdale's ordering six to eight dozen at a time." But all the baskets at the Basket Barn have the Alvey look — a distinctive basket design that basket collectors everywhere recognize and love.

Curtis says that baskets aren't used for much anymore, that they're just pretty objects. That may be true for some people. But I use his baskets, in all shapes and sizes, in every room of my home. I use them as decorative containers for flowers, fruit, breads, napkins, flatware, magazines, mail, makeup, toys — you name it.

For me, the handwoven basket will always

remain a work of art — made lovingly by hand, with great attention to detail — that can be appreciated both as a functional container and as an object of simple visual delight.

Years ago, everybody used to make baskets, especially on farms. They were very useful for many things — carrying corn, gathering eggs. People used them for market baskets, carrying corn cobs to build a fire. I just learned basket making growing up.

In the little community where I was from, there were a number of basket makers. When plastic and paper bags started coming in, people just forgot about baskets. But we held on, and in the last fifteen or twenty years, they've gotten popular again.

I read a piece in a magazine one time which said it's possible to make an oak basket by using an ax and a pocketknife. And basically, that's the main two tools we use. There's no machine. The only way you can cheat a little bit is by cutting the tree down with a chain saw.

The wood for baskets has got to be green. You start by cutting down a tree and splitting logs. All the work is done by hand. You take a piece of wood an inch thick and, instead of shaving the outside, you take your knife and open that wood up with the grain — it actually splits apart. You work it down and just keep going through the center each time until you get it down to the thickness you want. And that's what you make your framework with — your handle, your hoop, and then your ribs. You make your handle and hoop, then you tie them together with a wrap.

There are several different kinds of wraps. There's a rose tie, a dog leg, and many others. Then you start putting the ribs into that tie. After you get part of the ribs in, you start working the splits — you go all the way around, go to the top rib and right back again, over and under, all the way around. You do both sides that way and finally come together in the center.

You can spend three or four hours on a rough basket or you can spend three or four days on a fine-weave or collector basket. You can use a collector basket, it's durable enough, but so much time has gone into it that you want to keep it in its original condition. I often use baskets for gardening. As a matter of fact, I stumbled over a basket of sweet potatoes the other day and almost broke my neck! Still, white oak is a very durable wood. You can hose an oak basket down and keep it from drying out. Also, you can put either linseed oil or, preferably, tongue oil on it. Those will keep a basket from drying out. It's not unusual for an oak basket to last fifty or even a hundred years.

Lestel and Ollie Childress

Lestel and Ollie Childress and their nephew Clevie are regulars at practically every crafts show held in Kentucky. Lestel and Ollie are fifth generation basket makers from Hart County who have been making baskets together since before they were married. Their families were always very close and both had long histories of basket making.

Lestel and Ollie have made many baskets for me over the years. Their baskets come in all shapes and sizes, but the Childress baskets all have a distinctive design. Ollie made a special one with red splits when she found out red is my favorite color. The Childresses have made baskets for Marshall Fields in Chicago and for the "Oh! Kentucky" boutique at Neiman-Marcus in Beverly Hills.

Their fondest hope is that their grandson J.R. will join their nephew Clevie and his sons to ensure that a seventh generation of Childress basket makers carries on the proud tradition.

Ollie spoke with us one afternoon in her kitchen, surrounded by the fresh white oak Lestel had just carried in from their back-yard woodshed.

L estel and I have been married forty-three years but we've been making baskets together for over fifty years. My father died when I was six years old and my mother died when I was eleven. I had to go live with my sister Rachel who was married to Lestel's older brother George. Both Rachel and George made baskets, and Lestel and I used to work on one basket together. We'd put a basket frame in our laps and Lestel would work on one side while I worked on the other.

Lestel asked me to marry him when I was fifteen years old. I'll never forget my wedding dress. I bought a beautiful blue crepe dress at Lestel's grandmother's second-hand store. Aunt Lett, as everyone called her, was a legend in Hart County. She made baskets well into her eighties. She traded me that blue crepe dress for a peck basket I made for her. I was so proud of that dress. I'll never forget it.

Lestel's parents taught him how to make baskets. His dad peddled baskets by the roadway. Everybody in both our families made baskets. Up till recently, we made baskets all the time. We'd just sit right out there under the big apple tree in the front yard and make all kinds of baskets. When it got too cool, we'd just move into the kitchen.

When we want to make a basket, we go to the woods to look for a young, straight white oak between six and seven inches in diameter with no knots in it. Lestel carries the timber into the barn and takes his wedges and maul and busts the wood out.

He halves it, then quarters it. From that point on, he can take his froe and mallet to it. He removes the heartwood, the dark wood in the center of the tree, then he busts the white sap wood into small pieces about one-and-a-half to two inches wide. He does everything else with his pocket knife. Timber has a grain in it, and it should just peel apart if it's good wood.

We've taught an awful lot of people how to make baskets. We've been demonstrating our basket making at universities and crafts fairs now for over ten years.

The Kentucky Guild of Artists and Craftsmen sponsored a three-day white oak basket making workshop at Virginia Petty's farm. Virginia took the workshop, of course, and Sarah Frederick was there, too. Two of Kentucky's finest white oak basket makers, Beth Hester and her husband, Scott Gilbert, conducted it. We taught them to make white oak baskets .They're like family to us now. We're happy to share what we've learned over the years about making baskets with other craftspeople in Kentucky.

People often ask me how we make our colorful baskets. Lestel usually runs the splits and I dye them in a kettle on the stove. Then we just weave those dyed splits into our baskets.

Sometimes Lestel and I sit here making baskets for hours and we don't even say a word to each other. Other times, we'll sit here and talk about everything under the sun. We often listen to my gospel tapes while we're working. It's amazing what basket making can do for me. It calms me down and lifts my spirits

Lestel and I are fifth-generation basket makers and we feel it's important to preserve our family's tradition. I just hope that I live to see one of my grandchildren become a basket maker, so we can ensure that the seventh generation of the Childress clan stays in this important family craft.

151

M a r y   a n d   R o b i n   R e e d

Going to see Mary and Robin Reed in our four-wheel-drive Jeep was like taking a trip back in time. We topped a mountain, forded a creek, rounded a bend, crossed over a bridge, then arrived at their home in a beautiful valley in the Daniel Boone National Forest.

The Reeds are a versatile crafts couple who can make everything from baskets to weavings, from candles to cornshuck flowers and nativity scenes. And as anyone who has ever visited them outside Irvine, Kentucky, will tell you, their life-style is as interesting as their crafts and as much a part of their story.

Imagine two college-educated, middle-class people who sought an alternative — call it "hippie" if you like — life-style together twenty years ago, as many others did, but who have stayed committed to it ever since.

Mary and Robin live in a small Sears prefab home which has no electricity and no running water. But being with this happy family, you realize there is nothing missing

from their lives. They lead a peaceful, quiet, and natural existence. Sitting in their cozy kitchen, I couldn't help but wonder about all the appliances and conveniences we think we need to be happy.

In spite of their quiet life-style, the Reeds are an active family. In addition to running their busy home craft business, they conduct craft workshops through the public schools and library and the local craft cooperative. They have also worked with local television stations on programs about alternative life-styles and preservation. Mary finds time to be president of her children's PTA. Their daughter is an adorable tomboy who plays on a T-ball team who, in her uniform, reminded me of Tatum O'Neal in The Bad News Bears.

To keep up with their many family and work commitments, the Reeds are a two-car family, though it wouldn't have surprised me, when I first arrived at their house to have seen a covered wagon parked outside.

Mary and Robin are fully aware of the eccentricity of their style of life, especially in an age when most former hippies are "yuppies," and they acknowledge it with a laugh, as if to say, "We don't take ourselves all that seriously."

The Reeds pride themselves on being self-sufficient. Their young son proudly showed us the bucket of crawdads he had caught in their creek the day we visited, then set off to sell them at the general store for three cents apiece.

Their traditional country crafts are always popular at crafts fairs, but it is their Kentucky spirit we celebrate here — a stubborn resistance to the easy way out, a reverence for living off the land, and a love for making things with their hands.

ROBIN: We were both born and raised in Lexington, Kentucky, and we both went to the University of Kentucky. I was studying architecture and Mary was studying in the fine arts program.

Our first venture into crafts was candlemaking. My cousin, a candlemaker in California, moved back to Kentucky and was making candles in the basement of his farmhouse in Woodford County. He gave us ideas for what you can do with wax.

When we started, we didn't know anything about the craft business. A friend of ours turned us on to the first crafts fair. We started making money selling the things we'd made, but it was just subsistence level for many years. In about 1980 or '81 we started making a little more money because we started going to crafts workshops sponsored by the Kentucky Department of the Arts. We both had to learn the business and learn to get personal with the people we were selling to. Now we make a little more money each year.

We enjoy the isolation of living away

from the city. We were from middle-class families but we just gave it all up. Being college educated and "green" to the ways of the country, we turned to the local community for its knowledge of survival skills. We learned about farming with horses, cooking and heating with wood, preserving food, birthing and raising children, practicing herbal medicine, building houses, and of course making natural crafts. This has allowed us to survive and to gain total independence of thought and action.

I always have my eyes open for new basket designs. Mary and I read all kinds of magazines for ideas. We always try to stay abreast of what's happening in the Atlanta crafts show in the fall, when all the new designs, trends, and colors come out. We latch right on to those new colors and start dyeing our cornshucks those colors. By March, they move!

We work all day and all night, but we do most of our craft work after dinner. We take orders any time of the year. Other craftspeople like us are one of our biggest buying markets.

MARY: Candles were popular in the 1960s and '70s. But we stopped making our candles because they were just not exciting to people anymore. We've now gotten into about eight kinds of cornshuck flowers, dolls, nativity settings, and baskets. We buy cornshucks by the bale, already bleached and cut. They're very easy to work with. We used to go into town once or twice a month with our team of horses to pick up the cornshuck bales.

Joan Curry was the woman who taught me about cornshuck flowers. She lived in Lexington. I would take her some of my flowers and she'd tug at the petals and they would fall off. She'd say, "They're no good, take them back." That's the best thing she could have done for me. I developed my own style. The first cornshuck doll I ever made took me all day and I read the instructions out of *Mother Earth News*. As soon as I sat it down, it fell apart.

But there's a great camaraderie among craftspeople and we got a lot of help and advice from them at craft fairs. When we were making candles we would sit next to someone who made cornshuck flowers and they'd show us how to make them. We'd come back and say, "What do you think?" and they would tell us how to improve them.

People ask us why we live the way we do. We say, "How can we keep from living this way?" We can't turn away from the reasons why we moved here. Our creative spirit comes from living in the hills, and that spirit stays with you.

*M*etal

Charles Lane

Charlie Lane is a Kentucky craftsman who has studied and revived a traditional craft because of his sheer joy in doing it. Charlie is a pewtersmith — one of the few masters of the art left in America.

His creations are reproductions of the types of objects that were common to Colonial life — plates, porringers, goblets, mugs, candleholders. Our forefathers owned these things in abundance, but today Americans rarely use them and know nothing about how they were made.

Charlie didn't know anything about them either, but in 1965 he decided to learn. Searching for clues in books revealed very little. It was through a craftsman at Colonial Williamsburg that he found a mentor who agreed to teach him the tricks that he

had learned in the pewter-smithing trade.

Now, twenty years later, Charlie himself is the mentor, passing along the pewter-smithing craft to an apprentice in Louisville. Charlie wonders why there aren't more young artists willing to work with the metal. "Pewter is a very malleable metal," he says. "It is easy to work with and beautiful to look at. And from the standpoint of an artist going to contemporary design, it would be an excellent medium."

Charlie's pieces are beautiful creations, the perfect marriage of utility and aesthetics. When he stops making them, we will have lost a very precious resource.

Pewter is a beautiful metal, and it's easy to work with. I'm fascinated with the history of the importance of pewter back in Colonial days, when they didn't have china. It wasn't until about 1850 that pewter began to decline as the preferred utensils to have on your dining table. My starting in

pewter goes back to a trip that my wife and I took to Williamsburg, Virginia, and, shucks, that's got to be over twenty years ago. We saw a craftsman doing hand-hammered work with pewter, and I wanted to learn some more on my own. I couldn't find any written material at that time, though, because this was a craft that had been handed down from a father to a son, from craftsman to apprentice, not written down. It took a blooming pewtersmith four to five years of being an apprentice before he was able to do this. Then, several years ago, I met John Q. Groot of the Ford Museum, Dearborn, Michigan, from whom I learned the art and craft of pewtersmithing. He worked for the museum and made pewter pieces for the gift shop and also demonstrated in the museum for tourists. He had a shop at his home, and he'd let me observe and do a few things in the museum or in his workshop. After he saw that my interest was valid, we'd go to his shop after dinner and work maybe till ten that night. Then we corresponded. When I ran into problems,

I'd pick up the phone and call him.

I shape pewter with a leather-faced hammer or mallet. I've got a dozen of them for different jobs. Pewter is a malleable, soft metal compared to silver, so you don't really use a forceful, striking blow, but a tapping strike to form the metal and encourage it to go into the shape that you're after. And that's what you see in these bowls. As you're striking, you're actually smoothing out the metal, so there's not a lot of hammered lumps. If you'll notice those pieces there, there's a lot that shines on them. You can still see the hammered facets but they don't really reach out and grab you.

The only way I work is with the raw material and my hammers and my wooden molds. You'd be surprised at the number of molds I've made over the years: bowls, candlestick bases, porringers. There's not enough desire for a manufacturer to make molds when there're not enough people who know what to do with them. And you do need several molds to fit each of the projects you're going to be doing, you know. So you make your own mold, which is not a hard thing to do. And your hammers are important, too. Some of my handles are croquet sticks. The hammer heads are covered with leather when you work your metal.

I just borrow Early American designs and use the same method they did. That perfect form is just that. It really can't be improved upon.

There are no pewtersmiths to speak of today. Maybe a dozen or so, if that many. I have a young fellow who has been working with me for two or three years as an apprentice and, hopefully, he'll carry on the work when I'm gone.

S a n d r a   a n d   J e r r y
W a l l i n

Jerry Wallin, a master metalsmith for twenty-three years, and his wife, Sandra, a tinsmith, live in a small farmhouse just outside Warsaw, Kentucky. They have been married fourteen years and together they operate a custom ironwork business called Wallin Forge. "It takes two of us to make one person," Sandra says, laughing. "It takes both of us to do what we do."

Watching them do what they do is like taking a step back a century or so. Jerry uses traditional metalsmithing skills to custom make everything from door hinges and gates to more artistic pieces like woven-steel coffers, boxes, Windsor chairs, tables, chandeliers, and decorative grillwork. They also work with a variety of metals to create historical pieces reminiscent of those made in the Shaker villages of the 1800s.

Jerry is a self-taught history buff who started out making nails and hinges for restoration projects and state historical sites. He volunteered to participate in historical reenactments and still, with Sandra, participates in demonstrations at Shakertown in Pleasant Hill, Kentucky.

Sandra is a professional photographer who became a tinsmith after she married Jerry. With Jerry's help and historical knowledge, Sandra found the necessary tools of the tinsmithing trade — most over 100 years old — and set out to revive this lost art. Much of what she knows she has taught herself by copying borrowed antiques and by examining museum pieces. She makes everything from Christmas icicles to lanterns, candleholders, lamps, and napkin rings.

The Wallins lead a simple country life in a peaceful setting. They take the truck into town for necessities and spend weekends off cycling around the countryside or combing museums all over the country for new books on their art forms and for new objects they might want to reproduce.

They made each other presents for their tenth (tin) and eleventh (steel) anniversaries. Jerry shared with us that he started out making a bracelet for Sandra and ended up making a beautiful jewelry box to keep it in as well.

They are a crafts couple in every respect — working as a team doing crafts they love.

SANDRA: Jerry and I met when we were both working for the state. He is such a history nut — he really got me interested in history. I decided that instead of finding a job of some kind, I would rather be self-employed like Jerry has always been. That's how I got into tin.

We would go to villages like Greenfield Village up in Dearborn, Michigan, and watch people work, not just the tinsmiths, but anybody making something from scratch. There are no "how-to" books in this country on tinsmithing. There are only books that record historical tinware. You just have to find someone like the tinsmiths at Greenfield Village.

Tinsmithing was never just a hobby to us. We spent a year and a half just looking for tools. Nothing was cheap because they are very hard to find. When people say to me, "Gee, I wouldn't mind trying that," I say there's no way just to try tinsmithing. First you have to outlay thousands of dollars for your tools, then you have to try to find someone who will teach you how to do it, which is next to impossible. There are only about fifty tinsmiths in the entire U.S.

It's interesting — when we say "tin" now people often equate it with "cheap." We don't think of it as rare, expensive metal. Tinware before the 1800s was a metal of kings because it was a very silvery metal. The main ingredient in pewter is tin — that's why pewter is so expensive. When tin is the major element in anything, the price goes up because it is so rare.

I sell my pieces both to decorators and to individual clients. Many of them are restoring a house and they want me to do all the lighting. Historical sites and gift shops sell my things. There are a variety of outlets for my pieces. They can be used in both historical and modern settings.

JERRY: I feel as if I have always been doing this. There was no period when I actually learned how to do it. I just grew into it. There is no person I can point to to say, "He got me started," or "I saw this person do this and it looked interesting to me." I have no idea when I first started forging, but I have always been interested in history and that is what got me interested in blacksmithing in the first place.

One difference between Sandra's tinsmithing and my forging is the type of tools we use. I deal with heat — everything I do has to be forged. When I first go into the shop in the morning, the first thing I do is light the fire and get everything going. I may not even start forging anything, but I have to get the fire ready. It's important to have the coals just right. If it burns too long, you have to rebuild it.

I use a forge to heat the metal and an anvil to work it. I also have hammers and

tongs to hold onto the metal. I have all sorts of punches and chisels and different types of hammers to do different work. You need bending tools, swedge blocks, different tools to shape the metal. The tools just accumulate over time. You'll buy a tool, then you'll see something better and either buy it or trade an old tool off to get a new one.

In this business, you're always growing. I started out making nails for people. They would want nails for a restoration or for a certain cabinet piece that they were reproducing. They would want everything about the restoration to be authentic, so I would make all the nails, hinges, shutter hooks, and things. Then I started being creative and making things on my own. I would come up with an idea like a chair. I would make tables — large tables — gates, beds, chandeliers. The latest pieces I'm doing include a box of woven steel. I just wanted to experiment to see if I could weave steel. When the people at the Art and Craft Foundation saw it, they asked me if I could weave a waste basket out of steel. Sandra suggested I submit other designs for waste baskets as well, and we designed one that looks just like a grocery bag. It has all the crinkles and folds in it — just like a real paper grocery bag — but it is all steel.

That's the thrill of forging, really — coming up with new things. I will do something that is a one-of-a-kind piece and somebody will come to me with yet another idea that is fun to make. It's always different — that's the exciting part of this.

You couldn't do this alone — neither Sandra nor I can. Often one of us will have an order so big we take time away from our own work to help the other out. It takes both of us to run our businesses. It also helps, when one of us comes up with a new design, to have another person to work off of. We wouldn't want to do what we do by ourselves.

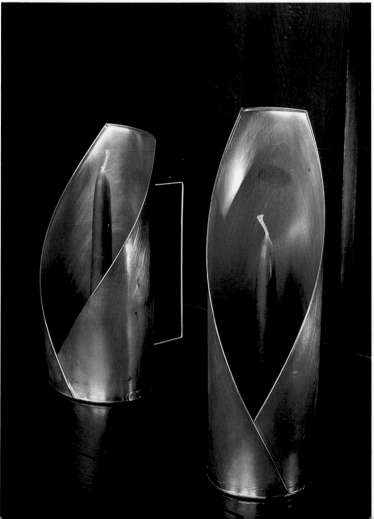

H a r r y   F u r c h e s

Harry Furches is one of those rare people whose living situation is a clear reflection of his artistic self. Harry and his wife live in far-western Kentucky, in Murray — home to Murray State University — where Harry has distinguished himself over the last twenty years as a metalsmithing professor and where he has gained a reputation as one of Kentucky's most imaginative silversmiths and jewelry designers.

His creative inspiration comes primarily from nature. He and his wife live in a home they commissioned Herb Green to design and build for them in a wooded area near Kentucky Lake. Harry's second love is racing sailboats, and many of his pieces reflect his love for water and waves. He even designed and built a sailboat with silver-inlaid trim which, unfortunately, was stolen and never recovered.

Harry's multilevel wooden home is a work of art. It has a floor-to-ceiling picture window which brings the surrounding woods inside. While we were visiting, a red-headed woodpecker munched on a platter of raw sunflower seeds on a deck outside that window, and it was easy to see how that beautiful, natural setting could inspire Harry to create his free-flowing jewelry designs and silver pieces.

Harry's silver teapots are exquisite works of art — each hammered and raised into an original design. They are displayed in museums in Kentucky and are sought after by serious silver collectors everywhere.

Harry is the son of a jewelry store owner and he has taught metalsmithing to his children. Like many Kentucky craftspeople, he is looking forward to retiring from his lifetime profession of teaching in order to devote full time to metalsmithing. He told us that he is going to outfit the studio behind his home to teach blacksmithing to his sons and to experiment with many of the designs he is accumulating in a "future ideas" notebook.

We can't wait to see where Harry's dreams will take him.

I have been a pretty lucky person in a lot of ways. Things just happened for me. I guess I just fell into them more or less without really thinking. I'm not a real thinker, I'm a craftsman. I have a feel for the technical excellence that it requires to be good at what I do. In spite of aesthetic directions, you really need to know a lot about technique in order to work. You have to be able to control the situation. Raising was something I always liked. If you can learn to raise a bowl, then

"In metalsmithing it's really helpful if you can draw. You can solve so many problems. When working with something as expensive as silver, it's a good idea to work it all out on paper beforehand."

you don't have to meddle with it, and that gives you a lot of technical skills. I learned raising myself, just by trial and error, basically. Raising is taking a large piece of silver which comes in sheet form — you buy it in sheets or pellets to cast it in any kind of thickness or dimensions you want — then simply hammering that metal and manipulating it to where you want it to be.

You use what we call a stake, which is just a form, and you hammer over that. If you start hammering on silver to raise it up or to change its shape, it gets very hard, so you have to heat it, to anneal it, to make it soft again. I raise the silver until I get it to a certain shape that I want, then hold it up and look at it, then hammer it a little more.

It's not very easily learned. Well, for a lot of people it's not. Some have a knack for

it. I do. I don't know why. I can't explain it. You're always going to learn some things by trial and error. If there weren't any errors, there wouldn't be any art. So by taking those things that are mistakes, and turning them into something that happens for you in terms of aesthetics — that's art.

To do metalsmithing, you have to be strong and you have to have patience, tenacity, and courage. If you're going to mount a stone on a piece of jewelry, you have to have the knowledge to be able to do it, but you also have to have the patience to sit there and do it in little degrees so you don't screw up. You don't turn something out unless you're satisfied with it — or else you go back and do it over.

Dad kind of assumed that I would take over his jewelry business. But, you know,

I think he respects my life the way I have done it. What I do comes naturally for me. I just really enjoy working with metal.

I wouldn't quit making jewelry pieces any more than I would give up sailing. It's just a part of me. A couple of my recent pieces have been a little more contemporary than my earlier, traditional pieces. I plan to go on in that direction when I retire. I'm doing larger pieces, too. Actually, I just want to experiment. I really haven't had the chance to do that. To do a large piece takes a lot of time. When I retire, I'm going to reestablish my studio out here and just make things, go to fairs, and travel all over.

I've got a sketchbook full of ideas I want to make into something. I'll just sit here and look at all those things and just let them come out as they want to.

Folk Art and More

M a r v i n   F i n n

Inside a modest home in the Clarksdale public-housing project in Louisville lives a small man with a huge imagination and a light-hearted sense of humor about life and everything in it.

Marvin Finn's kitchen workshop is a play-land of bright, painted birds, figures, toys, animals, trucks, cranes — whatever happens to be the latest whim and fascination of this very talented and popular wood-carver.

This man, who has become one of Kentucky's most famous folk artists, sits in the corner of his kitchen on a child's chair with a worn-out cushion — his band saw resting in a child's red wagon in front of him — carving creatures from sheets of plywood, and painting them in wild, exotic, sometimes fluorescent designs.

Marvin loves to laugh, finds humor in most things, and is almost disappointed if others don't find his crazy creations funny. Many of his latest animal inspirations — monkeys, baboons, penguins — come from frequent trips to the Louisville Zoo. Before the birds and animals, Marvin concentrated on intricately carved trucks, bulldozers, boats, and ten-foot-high cranes with working parts and crisscrossed toothpicks up and down their arms.

Marvin makes art out of other people's junk. His apartment contains a collection of "found" and "donated" treasures. For example, the afternoon I visited, I inquired about a long, V-shaped piece of scrap wood propped against his living-room wall. He giggled, which he does often, and told me that someday he would make the "biggest and best bird ever" out of that scrap wood. I challenged him to make that piece for my personal collection. Imagine my surprise and delight when I picked up the finished product — a truly one-of-a-kind, twelve-foot-high flamingo with a brightly painted

body, wearing a red hula skirt! Only Marvin could even have imagined it. I just love it.

I grew up in Alabama, and I worked hard all my life. All my life. I worked on a farm. I lost my mom when I was a little baby and my daddy raised us, just like I raised my kids. I lost my wife when Lisa was two years old. I marched my kids to school every day and I would go get them. I was just concerned about them.

I used to make toys for the kids for Christmas. I wish that just one of my kids would work with me, but I don't think my boys will ever do anything like this. See, I learned from watching my dad and I thought he was everything. I still feel the same way right today and he has been gone a long time. I'm glad my dad didn't give me anything. He worked hard and he taught me a lesson. The Good Book said if you don't work, you don't eat. I go by that.

I just do what my mind tells me to do. Maybe the good Lord plants these things in

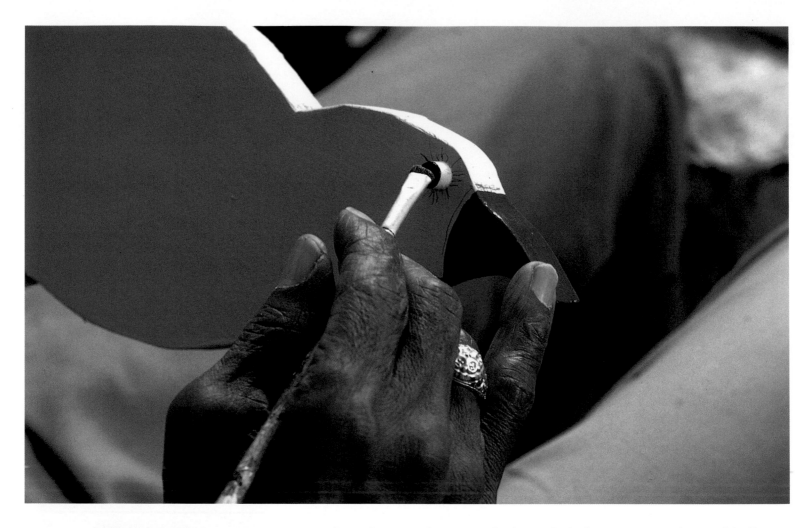

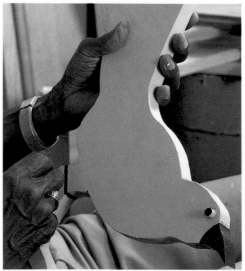

my mind, you know? When I go to bed, I have these things on my mind and I wake up with different things on my mind. Every day, I'm making something different.

I don't think people pay attention anymore. That's what gets me. You see something funny, you are supposed to laugh, right? That is what I try to tell people all the time. You see that baboon I'm making? I get a big kick out of it. I laugh nearly every time I look at it. Sometimes when I get lonesome I go out to the zoo to look for that baboon. I go to enjoy myself and laugh at him because he looks funny. I chew tobacco, you see, and I go out there and try to spit on that thing. And that dang fool, that spit gets to him and he'll jump right away. Oh, Lord, the funniest thing in the world is that big baboon.

I wish I was making money but I don't do this for no money. I do it because I like it. I still say, money ain't everything. What's wrong with this world is we need some love in this world. I don't care what nobody says. I say the good Lord is going to take care of me.

My mind tells me all the time that when I leave here and meet the good Lord, I ain't never going to quit making toys. That's what my mind tells me. That's heaven to me...making toys...and I look forward to it all the time.

S a l l y   C a m m a c k

On a hill above one hundred acres of rich Kentucky farmland, gourd artist Sally Cammack sits in her family room, creating the painted gourds that have made her one of Kentucky's best-known craftspeople. Her colorful gourds, with their distinctive scenes of country life in Kentucky, can now be found in the homes of crafts collectors in America, England, Europe, Africa, and Japan.

Sally and her son grow and cure gourds on her farm near Cynthiana, Kentucky.

Her store orders dictate how many gourds she'll choose from her garden and which of over a dozen country scenes she will paint. From then on it is a matter of drawing and coloring the scenes on the gourds and shipping them out to stores and other buyers. Sally's days, like all mothers', consist of getting children off to school and taking care of her family. When the house is finally quiet, she usually sits in a comfortable chair in her den, gourd and watercolor pen in hand, and works to complete the hundreds she always has on back order.

Sally's career in crafts began at about the time I first discovered and became interested in them. Guests at my Derby gatherings are always fascinated with Sally's work. When John was governor we often gave her gourds as gifts to dignitaries visiting Kentucky. In fact, I suggested that she try painting scenes on canvas rather than on gourds. Using some paint she had had for years and an inexpensive canvas she bought at a local discount store, Sally tried her first country scene canvas. She brought it to one of my

Derby parties, and Mrs. Henry Kissinger bought it. When people found out that the Kissingers had bought a painting from Sally, her work of course became even more widely recognized and valued.

Sally's gourds have an unmistakable style, but each is unique and each is a treasure.

I have always drawn. I liked to draw real small as a child. My mother would always fuss and say, "Make things bigger. Why do you have to draw them so little?" I just have always liked small things— small jewelry, small prints on fabrics. The smaller the better. And it's still that way with the gourds and the paintings. I found a way to use my talent for detail on small objects.

My mother-in-law developed the entire technique of gourd painting. She was a gourd fancier and had bought a carved gourd in Peru. She was trying to copy the Peruvian gourd and couldn't find a tool sharp enough to carve it, so she used an old

wood-burning tool and liked the results. She suggested I try it because she knew I liked to work with my hands. So I tried it and was pleased with what I did. That's still how I work on gourds. It's the same thing as a pen and ink sketch with a watercolor wash on paper. I outline the drawing on the gourd with a wood-burning tool, then add watercolors to it, then add two coats of varnish to seal it. Once this technique is applied, it looks like hand-tooled leather. Once you've put on the varnish — the soft

sheen — you have a completely different finish. It's still a little embarrassing when I tell people I work with gourds. They kind of roll their eyes and say, "Oh," thinking I make tacky crafts out of them.

My son has a gourd crop on our land, and I'll cure as many gourds from there as I can. The rest I'll get from Lena Braswell, who has a gourd farm in Georgia. She'll ship them up to me. And people give me gourds all the time. I get them from everywhere.

My painting style is just what it is. I would

love to be able to paint like Wyeth, but this is all I can do. I haven't had any formal art training. I played around with designs and color fields early on, trying to do what my mother-in-law was doing. But I didn't feel they were done well, so I moved to country scenes. I paint what I see every day in my normal surroundings. I was born in Stearns, Kentucky, a small town, and my "village" scene comes from there. I love small towns, and I'm always looking for houses and barns and new things to draw.

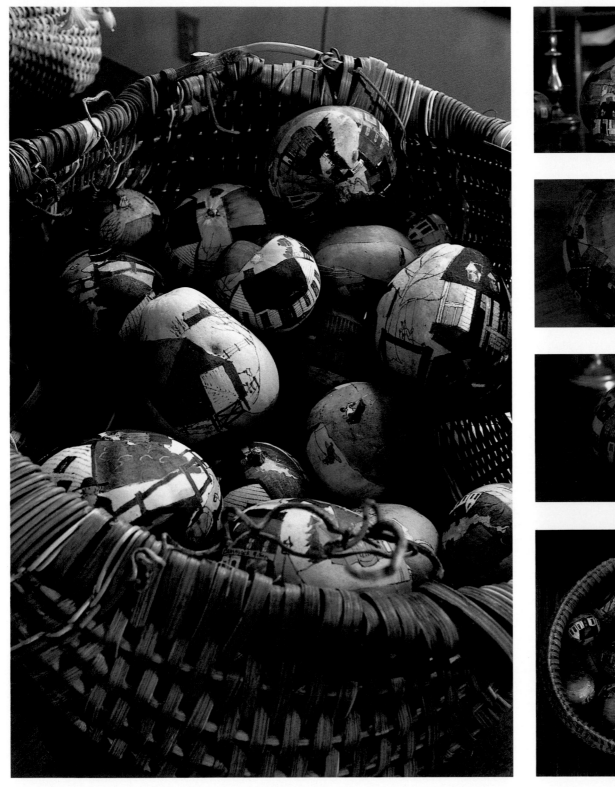

D e n z i l   G o o d p a s t e r

Denzil Goodpaster and his wife of sixty years, Lexie, live on a beautiful, breezy hilltop in eastern Kentucky, in a home with a perfect whittling porch. We spent a lovely summer afternoon together chatting in the bright red rocking chairs Denzil often sits in to carve elaborate canes and walking sticks.

Denzil was a farmer all his working life — the oldest son in a family of farmers who raised corn, beans, and tobacco in Morgan County, Kentucky. Denzil "had a little whittlin' stock" in his family, but he was most greatly influenced artistically by his mother, who, according to Denzil, "could make anything — even a house." Denzil always liked to whittle — "mostly shavings," he says — but he taught himself to carve "sticks," as he calls them, at the amazing age of sixty-two, when he retired from full-time farming.

Denzil's talents were first recognized when he sold his "sticks" at the local Sorghum Festival. He and Lexie, a wonderful quilter, shared a crafts booth there every year. Word of Denzil's unusual "sticks" spread rapidly in crafts circles and, with marketing and distribution help from his agent, Larry Hackley, Denzil's circle of admirers widened rapidly.

Denzil, now eighty, was ill for a while but is getting back to his carving. His "sticks" are imaginative and colorful — whimsical collector's items — brightly-painted carvings of snakes and frogs and alligators and fascinating human forms, all decorated with rhinestones and beads he has collected over the eighteen years he has been carving.

He has carved likenesses of Dolly Parton — one of his favorite entertainers — and of Minnie Pearl. Some of his canes seem inspired by Indian totems.

The day we visited, Lexie treated me to a private showing of her favorite quilts and of her springhouse filled with every kind of canned goods imaginable. Denzil donned his favorite cap and walked me down to his woodshed to show me his treasured collection of wood pieces — "sticks-to-be" — then showed me how he passes afternoons carving in the doorway of the shed.

It saddened me to think that Denzil and so many of Kentucky's older craftspeople are, indeed, a vanishing breed. When I asked Denzil why he thought today's young people aren't interested in carrying on the work of Kentucky's fine whittlers and woodcarvers, he replied, "Patience. They just don't have the patience."

We all left that day wishing we had more time in our own lives for the peaceful porch-sitting that has inspired generations of woodcarvers like Denzil Goodpaster.

"Sometimes I just sit out there in the door of my woodshed and whittle, then I go out early in the morning when it's cool to pick the shavings up. Lexie always makes me pick up my shavings."

I guess I make about one hundred walking sticks a year. I can make about one a day, and I've been making sticks for about eighteen years now. I still make them the same way I always have...with just a pocketknife. First I use a hatchet to get the wood down to size, then I use a pocketknife — a real sharp one.

The cheapest knives are the best ones. I've used a lot of different kinds and I still have the best one I've ever had. It cost six dollars. I use all the blades on it. I wouldn't have one with less than three blades.

I don't ever draw these things out before I start whittling. I just think 'em up. Sometimes, though, if I've seen a picture or something, I'll try to make a stick like it.

I whittle my sticks out here on this porch, and I go out under the shade of that tree when it's too hot.

I get my wood from a lot of different places. I'll pay for a pickup truck load of good wood. I only use oil paint. What paint I don't have, I just mix my others to get. I buy old costume jewelry for the eyes and things. I bought all this jewelry. People didn't know what it was, you know, and they'd sell it for nothing.

I've tried to teach a few young people how to do what I do, but they say they haven't got the patience. I reckon they thought they'd have to make one in just an hour or two. It takes longer than that.

I wish some young person would take up my job. I'll have to quit someday anyway. I may never make another one, I don't know. I don't really mind if people ask me to make the same stick over again. I don't care. The more I make of them, the better I am at making them. Just so long as I'm making them is all I care about.

Walking sticks from the collection of Larry Hackley

182

K u r t   L u d w i g

Kurt Ludwig has been making toys since he was five years old, but we just recently discovered his fantasyland of mechanized toys when we visited his home in Louisville.

Kurt is the brother-in-law of an acquaintance of mine, Jim Oppel, who is managing editor of Louisville Magazine; *and it was Jim who brought Kurt's incredible talent and toys to the attention of the staff at the Kentucky Art and Craft Foundation. The first pieces Jim took down to the gallery were well received and sold immediately. It is easy to understand why when you see them.*

They are mechanical wizardry and they bring out the child in all of us. You have to play with them when you see them, to discover the ingenious way each figure moves.

Despite his success and recognition, Kurt, like so many Kentucky craftspeople, still makes toys just because he loves to. Kurt is an estate gardener and landscaper by day and toymaking is a hobby to him, not a livelihood. "I price my toys by how much I'd have to charge to bear to part with them," he says, laughing. The only challenge in his craft is to devise even more elaborate toys — more figures, with more things going on.

Kurt lives in Louisville with his wife, Lila, an artist in her own right, and their three young children, Sarah, Daniel, and Andrew, the beneficiaries of his finest pieces.

Toys just have a special appeal for me. I don't know if it's because they were the first things I made, or if it's because there's a little boy in me.

I've been doing this virtually all of my life. I can remember making things when I was very, very young. I can remember being no more than five and sneaking my dad's saw and making boats out of scrap lumber that I found in the woods out back of our house. When I got too old to play with the things I had made, I would make things for my little sister. There has always been somebody to make them for — now I make them for my kids.

The things I make now are just the things that come into my head. I cannot make something without at least a couple of new ideas coming into my head that I really have a strong urge to make. The mechanics really interest me because I enjoy watching the movement. It is a real challenge to get things to work the way I want them to. I like the diversity. I like to do things that I haven't seen before.

It does take a lot of patience. It can take me a long time to figure out how to get something to work right and to work in conjunction with something else. It is also

184

hard to get timing down. It is one thing to get something to do a certain action, but to get it to do it at the proper time in relation to another figure does take a lot of patience. The more work I do, the more I learn about how to make things do certain things. I figure out what I want a figure to do and what I want to have the theme be, and then I decide if there is a way to do it. It is kind of backwards. Rather than figure out the mechanics first, I figure out what I want the people to do. I hope to get more complex as I go, to have my pieces do more things, to have several axles going at once. The things I would like to do in the future, when I have more time, are going to take more than one main axle to do the things that I want them to do. I am just interested in action and reaction movement.

I feel like everything I make has sort of a toy quality about it. It's not that I set out to make a toy or that I set out to make a piece of art. I just get these ideas and that's what I end up making. I think a toy can be art and craft and mechanical, and I don't think these have to be separate divisions. I think they can all go together. And I hope, with at least some of my things, there is some mingling of the three.

All my life I've had sort of a conflict about whether what I'm doing is what I should be doing. I sometimes hear, Why are you wasting your time with that? Why don't you do something really worthwhile?

My time for this is extremely limited. I work a regular job. I'm an estate gardener and I work a lot of hours on my own landscaping. I've got family responsibilities, a house to keep up, and all those other things. So I find if I get into a big project, something that's going to take a long time, it may be years before it's finished. I do have ideas on the back burner — things that I consider a little more serious that

show more emotion or are a little more elaborate, that show facial animation and more expressive body movement of people, animals, whatever. These ideas are on hold for the moment.

There's one project in particular that I'm really excited about doing someday, but it's got in excess of a dozen-and-a-half people, plus other actions going on at the same time. It's a stage, with a band, with the fiddler actually fiddling, the banjo player actually playing banjo, the guitar player actually playing the guitar, and dancers. I've gone through these ideas in my head a hundred times and I know exactly how to make the people do what I want them to do. I've got an old man on the side with his cane going up and down, slapping his knee; a lady bouncing her baby; several different couples, not just spinning around, but doing different things. A bashful boy being pushed toward a little girl he wants

to dance with — just all sorts of things going on at this sort of country jamboree. It will take a very, very long time to make.

I figured out a long time ago that it would be hard to make a living making toys. But craftsmanship is more appreciated now than it was a number of years ago. I think you, Phyllis, and the Kentucky Art and Craft Foundation have had something to do with that. Particularly Kentucky crafts, it seems, but crafts in general and rudimentary art like I do seem to be more respected. People don't laugh at my things or say, well, that's stupid. They say, this is an investment. This is art.

I know this may be hard to believe, but if I had no hope of ever selling something, of having anybody ever see it, if it were taken away completely from me as soon as it was finished, and I never saw it again, if I got no reward from it whatsoever, I would still make it.

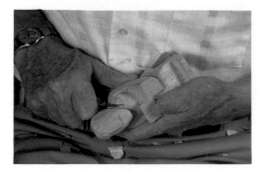 

U n t o   J a r v i

Born in Finland, but for many years a resident of Auburn, Kentucky, Unto Jarvi is one of a number of Kentucky folk artists who began his career as a wood carver and landscape painter after he retired from the construction trades at the age of sixty-two. "Fifty years was enough," he says.

Unto is perhaps best known in Kentucky for his intricately carved dioramas, each a depiction of earlier, pioneer days, which he calls "the old life."

Now eighty years old, Unto will proudly tell you that his pieces are in public and private art collections in thirty-eight states and five countries. The people in the Upper Peninsula of Michigan, where he spent many summers, are so fond of his work that they declared Unto Jarvi Day in Michigan.

Unto hopes to revive pleasant memories for his own generation with his dioramas, and to acquaint present and future generations with the hardships their ancestors withstood making a better life. Each diorama is a three-dimensional setting of room furnishings, or of an outdoor scene into which Unto places "Jarvi's Little People" — his own affectionate term for the unusual characters he carves with his pocketknife. Each of his figures has unique features and costume and exhibits the particular emotions he is trying to convey. Many typically show tears, Unto's way to show that life for these people — very much like his own — was hard.

Unto has taught himself to do many things in life. He taught himself a variety of construction skills which he called upon to build his own home in Auburn and the homes of many of his relatives there. He taught himself to carve and to paint when he was injured on a construction job and, upon his retirement, chose to pursue his hobby on a full-time basis.

Even at eighty, Unto is a tall, imposing man — broad-shouldered and muscular from years of hard labor. There is a warmth and sensitivity about this man, however, which shows in his works and which was particularly evident to us when he spoke of his wife and helpmate, Beatrice, who passed away a few months before we visited. In fact, when he picked up his favorite pocketknife and carved features on a figure while we were there, he shared with us that it was the first time he had felt like carving since Beatrice had passed away.

I loved every minute I spent with Unto in western Kentucky and especially enjoyed viewing the "little people" and dioramas he keeps in a studio he has constructed behind his house. I couldn't resist purchasing a few of his pieces, my favorite being an intricately carved diorama of the Last Supper, entitled "...and his Disciples." I take great pride in knowing that I can always keep Unto's memory and talent alive by enjoying these unique pieces and by later passing them on to museums and appreciative collectors.

When I was sixty-two, I said, "I've worked fifty years in the construction industry and I'm no richer, so I'm going to quit." I came home and said, "I am going to quit." My wife said, "You mean you are going to quit?" And I said yes, and that was it.

I did my first carving eighteen years ago at age sixty-two, and I have been doing it ever since then. I'd whittled spoons, but I had never tried carving a figurine. It didn't surprise me that I could do it. I made a lot of them. I did hundreds of carvings.

The first diorama I made was of a store-keeper slicing a ham, and there was a woman and a man in it with oversized rear ends so I called it "Kentucky Hams." I sold it to a place that sold hams.

Then I had a show at Western Kentucky University. I received a grant from the National Endowment for the Arts. They seemed to like my work, maybe the ideas in my work. You see, each of my dioramas tells a story about life. I didn't know what life could be like when it was easy-going. It was always hard-going. I always had a hard life. What I like to do is show what it was like when I was growing up back in the twenties and thirties.

My parents were hard-working people. My father came to the United States a long time before the rest of us did — for five years we didn't know if he was living or not. We came to this country when I was eleven years old. I went to school here for a while, but soon I had to go to work. We had it pretty rough then. We hacked a farm out of the wilderness, living in a small shack with my mother and two sisters.

My mother was a very religious person. She was hard on the kids, very hard, very strict — so strict that I left home to work in a logging camp when I was thirteen years old. But my mother could look at something somebody had made, and she would

187

"You don't learn to do things from books. You learn from experience, and I have done many things in my life. I carved my first figure at age sixty-two."

say, "Oh, I can do this just by looking at it." And she could.

If someone commissioned me to make something, I wouldn't do it at all. I don't like to make something that somebody tells me to make this or that way because, you see, that isn't mine. I didn't really do that piece. It is like a painting. If I were to copy from a photograph, I wouldn't say that was my painting. All my paintings I do from memory. I don't copy them.

I appreciate that people admire my work, but I don't see anything special about it. To me, it comes so easy that it is relaxing. I'm not doing this for the money. I don't make three dollars an hour on a lot of it. But that's all right. It doesn't matter to me one bit.

189

"Water Boy"   garvi

"Rest Stop"   Jarvi

Jarvi

Bonnie Lander

Bonnie Lander is a young, city-born artist who now lives with her writer/photographer husband and their two children on one hundred beautiful acres near Bethlehem, Kentucky. Her specialty is bright, colorful country scenes painted on a variety of objects — traditional canvas, gourds, saws, eggs, walls, barns, ax handles. or anything else she takes a fancy to. Hers is a talent both for painting the scene and for playfully adapting its details to the various surfaces she selects.

Of all the objects Bonnie paints, her gourds have become the most well known in Kentucky. She has developed a signature style that is recognized by many collectors.

A self-styled "detail freak," Bonnie is obsessive about the completeness of the scenes she paints. A large gourd, for example, will eventually be covered with an entire village of activity. A 360-degree turn of the gourd is like reading a book! But that is the appeal of her gourds — there is always a new view to appreciate.

Bonnie's productivity has been limited lately by the birth of her second child. "I'm really looking forward to getting back to it," she says. And we Bonnie Lander fans are looking forward to that, too.

My mother and father had a big garden and grew gourds one year, about eight or nine years ago. I was just absolutely fascinated with those gourds. My mother said, "What am I going to do with all these gourds?" And I said, give me one and for the heck of it I'll just paint it. I painted a little doll on it. Someone saw it and ordered ten or fifteen from me, and just that fast I started a business. I loved the way it felt. It was just something I could do. The gourds were so little, that it finally became a real challenge

But then I got tired of doing the dolls, and I thought I have got to do something else with these gourds. I had been doing little primitive canvases, and I thought, why not put one on a gourd? That was basically it. Someone saw them and went berserk over them, and I thought, well, why don't I stay with this? I just liked it, I enjoyed it. Everybody still gives me grief, saying "Why don't you paint on canvas?" I just don't want to! I've done canvases, and they're not a challenge like the gourds are.

I think what is so fascinating about gourds, at least to me, is that I can get bored with one side of them and just turn them around. It's like looking at something new. I paint my gourds to death. I never know when to quit.

Did you notice there are no fuel-powered or steam-powered or motor-powered vehicles in any of my drawings? There is a wagon and a horse, or a sled, or people working in the garden, or people ice skating on a pond or fishing on a pond. It's all what I find romantic. I think we have become so absolutely mechanized and technological in everything in this country and I'm sick of it. That is why I'm out here in the country.

"I love detail. I paint my gourds to death. I keep adding and adding. I think it comes from living out in the country where the colors are so much more vibrant."

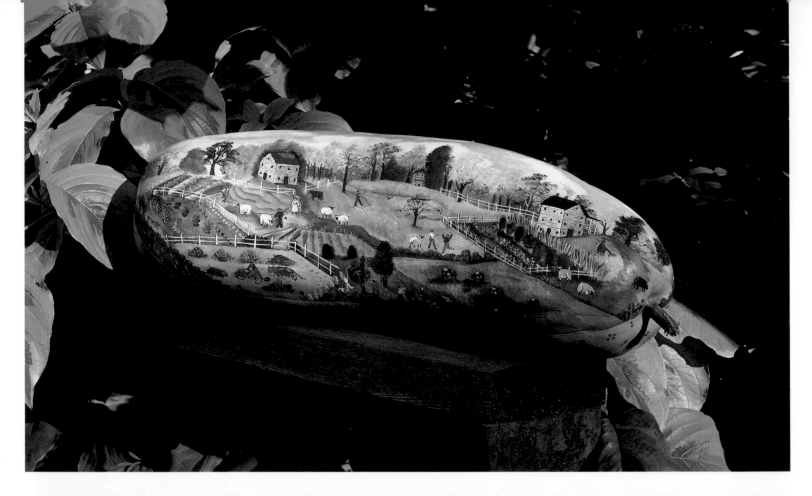

Carl McKenzie

Carl McKenzie is a Kentucky original. He and his wife of fifty years, Edna, live in eastern Kentucky on the edge of the Daniel Boone National Forest. After a life of farming, coal mining, and truck driving, Carl turned his attention to wood carving and whittling. In a short time he caught the attention of collectors and art historians with his highly imaginative figure carvings. Their spontaneity and natural expressiveness create a playfulness that is irresistible.

Carl himself is a character. At eighty-three he is as productive as ever, and full of life and humor. He is very interested in music, and showed me how to play "My Old Kentucky Home" on a saw and on a home-made instrument Carl calls a "tingin' bow."

The day I visited, Carl proudly showed me

his latest creation: "A man to take care of Edna after I'm gone." That "man" had a gun strapped on one hip and a knife on the other; a Bible in one hand and a bottle of Old Crow in the other — a mountain original, carved by a mountain original.

I sat on the porch with Carl and Edna on a hot Kentucky summer day as coal and logging trucks stirred the air nearby.

I was born in Pine Ridge, Kentucky, in 1905. I've been carving since I was a kid, making animals and little toys. I wasn't too good at it. I was too busy making a living. I've done just about everything. I worked on a farm over here in the Red River Gorge in 1918. My mother died when I was thirteen years old. From then on I just made my own way.

My father had worked for a lumber company. I was only seven when he was killed. There was two of them that were killed together. A storm come up and they tried to run for shelter, but they were both killed by a bolt of lightning.

I worked in a coal mine around Hazard, Kentucky, for ten years. When I quit the coal mine, I came back up here to my home country, and I drove a truck for a lumber company for seventeen years.

But all this time I was whittling, making nothing but shavings. I enjoyed it. My grandfather showed me how to use a knife. He made wooden dolls like I do. He wasn't too good at it. He was like I was when I first started it.

I don't know where my ideas come from. I just pick up a piece of wood and look at it, and I will think of something that I will make out of it. It amazes me.

All I ever use is a knife and a hatchet to rough things out before I start carving. Sometimes I use a saw for the big pieces. I guess I've gone through around a hundred knives since I've been carving.

I carve everywhere. I sit down yonder in the shade. I sit here on the front porch. The reason I don't carve on my back porch is 'cause I don't got a back porch!

Pieces from the collection of Larry Hackley

It takes about two days to make a figure, depending on how hard the wood is. I usually use white cedar. But it depends on what I'm making. I can work sometimes two weeks before I get one made. And whatever kind of paint I've got a lot of, that's what I use on my figures.

I just sit here on my porch watching the cars go by. But my eyes are failing me from looking at women. As they drive past my house, the old ladies smile at me, and the young ladies laugh out loud.

"I live here because this is the place I like best. I met my wife right here on this porch. I saw her sitting on the porch and I stopped to get a drink of water. That was an excuse; I didn't want no water!"